Kimono
きもの
日本語 Level 2

Suzanne Burnham
with Yukiko Saegusa
and Michael Sedunary

Illustrated by Alex Jankovic

Consultants
Robyn Spence-Brown
Junko Glynn

Produced with the assistance of
The Japan Foundation

TAVISTOCK COLLEGE
30/ 06/ 05

CIS·Heinemann
A division of Reed International Books Australia Pty Ltd
22 Salmon Street, Port Melbourne, Victoria 3207
Telephone (03) 9245 7111
Facsimile (03) 9245 7333
World Wide Web www.hi.com.au
Email info@hi.com.au

Offices in Sydney, Brisbane, Adelaide and Perth.
Associated companies, branches and representatives around the world.

2006	2005	2004	2003	2002		
20	19	18	17	16	15	14

Edited by Curtis Watson
Designed and typeset by Josie Semmler
Illustrated by Alex Jankovic
Additional illustrations by Bill Farr
Crane character by Randy Glusac

Colour separations by Excel Graphic Arts Company
Printed by Craft Print International Ltd

National Library of Australia Cataloguing-in-Publication data

Burnham, Sue.
Kimono. Level 2.

ISBN 0 949919 81 0.

1. Japanese language – Textbooks for foreign speakers – English.
I. Saegusa, Yukiko. II. Sedunary, Michael. III. Title.

495.682421

Contents・もくじ

第一課
おみやげです。
どうぞ。

Communicative tasks
Giving a self-introduction
Asking and saying what you
do in your spare time
Asking and saying where
activities happen
Giving and accepting
compliments

Situations and vocabulary
After the summer holidays
Self-introductions
Leisure activities
Places to do things

Language points
じこしょうかい expressions
(ーねんせい、すんでいます)
で to show place
じょうず、とくい
...ちゃん

*Cultural and linguistic
background*
Information on おみやげ,
pachinko and borrowed words
Writing ひらがな

第二課
Maiku くんはどこ?

Communicative tasks
Inviting someone out
Accepting, declining and
deferring invitations
Making a phone call
Asking and telling what people
are doing now
Describing yourself and others

Situations and vocabulary
On the phone
Invitation expressions
Parts of the body
Adjectives

Language points
...ませんか as an invitation
Physical characteristics
い and な adjectives
ています

*Cultural and linguistic
background*
A letter

カタカナ
Reading and writing カタカナ

第六課
ベビーシッター は
らくだなあ!

Communicative tasks
Asking permission
Giving and refusing permission
Saying what you are not
allowed to do
Talking about how much you
like or dislike something

Situations and vocabulary
Baby-sitting
Colours
Household items

Language points
...てもいいですか。
...てはだめです。
すきじゃない、きらい

*Cultural and linguistic
background*
High technology products
アンケート (Tokyo Disneyland)

第七課
この いす の あし は
ありますか。

Communicative tasks
Asking and telling where
things are
Shopping:
- asking what is available
- asking how much things cost
- deciding what to buy
- calculating the price

Situations and vocabulary
At the garage sale
Shops, and products, including
fruit, vegetable and stationery
items
Expressions for shopping

Language points
place にあります/です。
...はありますか。
－や suffix for shops
Counters つ、さつ、本
...を ください。
Numbers 1000 to 10 000

*Cultural and linguistic
background*
Japanese food
うた － かぞえましょう
Accentuate the positive－
focusing on positive reading skills

第八課
はし が つかえますか。

Communicative tasks
Asking and saying what you
are able to do
Asking and telling what
implements you use
Saying what language or script
you use

Situations and vocabulary
In the classroom
Implements for writing and
eating

Language points
...られます、...えます
できます
implement / tool で
language で
...へ *to (a place)*

*Cultural and linguistic
background*
Travel in Hokkaido

Introduction ・ はじめに

きもの 2 continues the lively, humorous approach to communicative language teaching adopted in the first level of the course. きもの 2 uses all of the communicative modes — listening, speaking, reading and writing — in a wide variety of activities.

The course emphasises language for use while taking a realistic approach to the need for carefully planned and clearly expressed grammatical explanations. Students are offered a great deal of communicative language supported by a systematic study of the structure of the language. In this way the course caters for a wide range of learning and teaching styles.

きもの 2 takes account of the increased language competence and the overall intellectual and social development of students of Japanese at this level. In きもの 2 Japanese language is used more extensively, most noticeably in the cultural units, which use material reproduced from magazines and brochures. Furthermore, there is more flexibility in the structure of the book and a wider variety of language presentations and activities.

きもの 2 therefore represents the continuation of a proven method and format with refinements and developments designed to meet the changing needs of the maturing Japanese learner.

The Japanese script

In きもの Level 1 students learnt to read and write hiragana and a small number of kanji characters. Writing is seen as an integral part of the きもの course and in きもの Level 2 katakana, and more kanji, are presented.

Katakana is introduced in a section at the end of Unit 2 of the textbook. A more detailed introduction to katakana, with ample opportunity for practice, is provided in the workbook.

Sixteen kanji characters are also systematically introduced in the workbook. Many of these characters have been chosen for their frequency of use. It is suggested that the characters be taught prior to the commencement of each unit so as to maximise student recognition and use. The use of furigana has been limited to the vocabulary section of each unit.

The きもの 2 Textbook

The きもの 2 textbook comprises the elements outlined below.

まんが

The full-colour まんが at the beginning of each unit introduce students in a stimulating way to the language contained in the unit. The storylines combine humour and fantasy, giving incentive to become involved in the activities which follow.

As a teaching tool the まんが are particularly useful as a fund of knowledge to be exploited in both oral and written exercises. For these purposes the まんが need to be broken down into manageable sections and even a single cartoon frame could be used for pronunciation practice, role-playing, to illustrate a grammar point, or as a jump-off point for the creation of original dialogues.

いいましょう

The いいましょう exercises focus on particular language points, enabling intensive oral practice using the visual information provided.

In きもの 2 these exercises are designed for whole class, small group and pair work. Some いいましょう exercises provide for more than one 'correct' answer; this encourages students to consider their given responses.

The いいましょう exercises are also used at times to present vocabulary, and familiarity in advance with the new vocabulary will ensure that maximum benefit is gained from these exercises.

Students should find these exercises interesting and purposeful and a useful preparation for further oral activities.

Ideas for exploiting the いいましょう exercises are contained in the teacher's manual.

ともだちと

These pair-work exercises are the next stage towards unstructured conversation. Students are required to make a series of choices of words or phrases to construct a coherent dialogue. This process of deliberately selecting elements of dialogue gives students insights into the flexibility of discourse and into the way in which it is constructed.

いってみましょう

This oral activity is a most challenging and rewarding opportunity for students to put the language acquired in each unit to real communicative use. In this phase the task is relatively unstructured and students are expected to produce appropriate language.

In きもの 2 extensive use has been made of survey sheets, profiles and original materials in an effort to make these activities as interesting and as real and purposeful as possible.

Teachers play an important role in ensuring the success of these activities, by providing adequate preparation and by supporting and encouraging students in some quite challenging situations.

日本語ノート

This section aims to provide a simple, clear explanation of the language covered in each unit. Its role is to systematise certain aspects of grammar in a straightforward manner building on what students already know.

がんばれ

These sections are included in Units 1, 3, 5 and 7. The articles are intended to provide students with strategies for 'learning how to learn' and for coping in real language situations.

The articles are intended for discussion, a starting point for the sharing of learning hints and for reference. They should be dealt with in an order that best suits individual classes.

たんご

As students become exposed to more and more language the task of organizing the acquisition of vocabulary becomes more complex. On one hand students need to be taught not to be too dependent on vocabulary lists. On the other hand a good range of vocabulary is a critical part of second language acquisition.

Some words and expressions that are included in this book and the workbook are intended for recognition and comprehension rather than for formal learning. This applies to many 外来語「がいらいご」used in the せいかつ and カタカナ sections of the workbook, and some footnoted items.

Vocabulary related to the main focus of the unit is presented towards the end of the unit. A variety of presentations has been used to avoid intimidating lists of words and expressions.

As with きもの 1 all vocabulary lists are arranged in the order of the Japanese syllabary chart, and Japanese-English and English-Japanese vocabulary lists appear at the end of the book.

せいかつ

The きもの course aims to integrate language studies with socio-cultural content.

The continuation from きもの 1 of the presentation of material via a series of letters from a young foreign student living in Japan is supplemented in きもの 2 by varying formats to introduce cultural insights. Some units present authentic brochures while others also present further cultural information in Japanese — this exposes students to the lifestyles of young people in modern Japan.

These sections can be used as starting points for further research or project work if desired. Exercises and ideas for follow-up activities are contained in the workbook and teacher's manual.

きもの 2 Workbook

The workbook accompanying the きもの 2 text contains a full range of exercises and activities which are designed to provide a thorough consolidation of the language points raised in the text. Its elements are outlined below:

ききましょう — listening comprehension exercises, the texts of which are spoken on the きもの 2 cassettes and written in the teacher's manual;

れんしゅうしましょう — contains a wide range of exercises and activities to provide mainly written reinforcement of the language content of each unit;

日本について — exercises and activities exploiting and extending the cultural material in each unit;

カタカナ — a comprehensive unit introducing the カタカナ script and reinforcing it via a variety of exercises and activities;

かんじ — the characters are given with their readings, definitions and stroke order. The readings given are those within the scope of the textbook.

きもの 2 Teacher's Manual

An invaluable resource for the teacher, this manual includes the elements below:

· the きもの method — an expanded discussion of points raised in this introduction;
· teacher's notes — how to use and exploit to the fullest all of the individual items in the course; how to use the course in class; sample lesson plans and guidelines for assessment;
· unit-by-unit analysis — includes a summary of the language presented, content of cassettes, suggestions for presenting each いいましょう exercise, scripts of listening comprehension activities, ideas for games and cultural units and some further language use explanations for teachers;
· reproduction masters — includes reading comprehension passages, sample tests for each unit and cartoon pages with separate listings of speech bubbles;
· photocopiable student progress sheets — provide students with the opportunity to assess positively their own progress.

きもの Cassettes

For each unit of the course, the cassettes contain:

· an entertaining recording of the まんが presented by young native Japanese speakers, both at normal speed and with pauses for repetition;
· a presentation of each いいましょう exercise;
· listening comprehension activities to accompany the ききましょう section of the きもの 2 workbook;
· a song and other items of interest in Japanese.

Acknowledgements

The publishers wish to thank the following organizations and people who contributed to the preparation of this book:

- The Japan Foundation Japanese Language Institute, for their generous financial support;
- Mr S. Kawate, Principal of the Noshiro North High School, for his cooperation and assistance;
- Dr and Mrs T. Kogure, Mr T. Sakaiya, the Ishida and Midorikawa families, Mr T. Matsuyama and Akiko Fujimori, for their assistance and hospitality;
- Katsuyuki Suzuki, Peter Burnham and Bill Farr for their general assistance;
- Toorak College, for its support.

The publishers also wish to acknowledge the following people who supplied photographs appearing in this book: Suzanne Burnham, Sumio Kawate, Sergio Montalban, Therese Hannan, Leanne Howard and Jacqui Beveridge.

Finally, the publishers gratefully acknowledge the companies who kindly gave their permission to use copyright material in this book. Despite every effort, the publishers were not always successful in tracing all copyright owners. Should this come to the attention of the copyright owners concerned, the publishers request that they contact them so that proper acknowledgement can be made in any reprint of this book.

きもの

viii

第一課・おみやげ です。どうぞ。

やすみは どう でしたか。

よかった です。かぞくと やまで kyanpu を しました。

ああ そう、ぼくは Hawai に いきましたよ。

あ...あのこ、だれ...?

みなさん、おはよう。ちょっと しずかに して...

あたらしい ともだち を しょうかい します。Maiku くん です。Maiku くん、じこしょうかい を してください。

Maiku です。十五さい です。Supootsu が とくい です。きょねんの saafin たいかいの chanpion でした。

それから、basuketto booru も とくいです。Ooru-sutaa chiimu の せんしゅです。どうぞ よろしく。

すごい! かっこいい! すてき!

ほんとうかなあ? うそ!

はい、Maiku くん、ありがとう。
じゃあ、そこに すわって。

ゆうこさん、日本 は どうでしたか。

おもしろかった
です。

あら? はなこさん は?

わたし は みね はなこ です。
ちゅうがく 三ねんせい です。
かいもの が とくい です。
ひまな とき へや で famikon を
します。どうぞ よろしく。

はなちゃん、
やめて!

みなさあん、おげんきですか。

だれ ですか。

それはなんですか。

おみやげです。
はい、どうぞ。

わあ! すごい! すてきな とけい...
どうも ありがとう。どこ で
かいましたか。

ありがとう! おもしろい
おみやげ ですね。

とうきょう dizuniirando
で かいました。

せんせい、おみやげ
です。どうぞ。

わたしに?ありがとう。

ねえ、ぼく には?
おみやげ...

あのこ、だれ?

Maikuくん です。Saafin
がじょうずですって。

ええと...

そうだ!

これ...Maikuくん に ちょうどいい
です。どうぞ。

どうも ありがとう。

わあ! Maikuくん、かっこいい!

いいましょう 一

（一）　（二）　（三）

Using the example as a guide, talk about the pictures.

例：

> A ひまなとき なに を しますか。
> B Gitaa を ひきます。

（四）　（五）　（六）

Using the example as a guide, talk about the pictures.

例：

> A ひまなとき なに を しますか。
> B Earobikusu を します。
>
> A どこ で?
> B たいいくかん で します。

Using the pictures as a guide, praise these people on their abilities.

例：

> A Erekutoon が じょうず ですね。
> B いいえ、そう でも ない です。

いいましょう 二

例:

どこ で たべましょうか。
ここ で たべましょう。

例:

どこ で たべましょうか。
そこ で たべましょう。

例:

どこ で たべましょうか。
あそこ で たべましょう。

一

二

三

例:

A どこ で たべましょうか。
B ここ で たべましょう。
　 or
　 そこ で たべましょう。
　 or
　 あそこ で たべましょう。

ともだちと

Make up a conversation with a partner.
Decide who will be A and who will be B.

A	あっ、	それは	おもしろい	T-shatsu とけい posutaa	ですね。

B	そう ですか。あたらしいです。		Hawai やま Rokku-konsaato	で かいましたよ。

A	だれと	Hawai やま Rokku-konsaato	に いきましたか。

B	はは かぞく ともだち あね あに	と いきました。

A	Hawai やま Rokku-konsaato	で	すいえい saafin dansu saikuringu kyanpu	を しましたか。

B	ええ、	たのしかった つまらなかった よかった	です。	[A] さん [A] くん	は	しゅうまつ やすみ にちようび	に なに を しましたか。

A	わたし ぼく	は	まち へや ともだちの うち にわ	で	famikon を しました。 CD を ききました。 えいが を みました。 いぬ と あそびました。 まんが を よみました。

いってみましょう

一 CD を どこ で かいますか。

Where is the best place to buy CDs or jeans or hamburgers?
Choose an item, such as one of the three above, and conduct a survey to find out where your classmates shop. Ask ten friends.

When you have completed your survey, you will be able to say which is the most popular shop among your friends.

Your survey form could look like this:

Survey on jiinzu	
なまえ	place
Robaato くん	Jeans City
Piitaa くん	Jac'n Jean
Maiku くん	Denim Heaven
Ben くん	Jac'n Jean

二 ひまなとき なに を しますか。

How well do you know your friend? Write down 6 statements (in 日本語 of course!) about what you think your friend does in her free time. She will also write down 6 statements. Ask her if she does what you have written. You can see how well you know her by the number of matching statements.

You may like to start by writing this:

Anさん は ひまなとき CD を ききます。   はい   いいえ

When you ask Anne, don't forget to put か on the end to make a question.

Here is a score sheet to check your friendship.

6	You know your friend very well.
5	You are good friends.
4	You know her quite well.
3	You have lots more to discover about your friend.
2	It should be fun getting to know her better!
1	Anne who?

三 じこしょうかい

じこしょうかい are used when you find yourself in a new situation and you need to introduce yourself. You might, like Maiku くん, be a new student to the class.

In Japan, じこしょうかい are used at school club meetings or scout meetings. They are also essential for writing to a pen-friend and for introducing yourself to new friends during a school visit or a home-stay. The content can vary according to the situation.

Listen to these students introducing themselves. You can use these examples to prepare a じこしょうかい for yourself.

一

わたし の なまえ は ふじもりまりこ です。なごや に すんで います。いま 十四さい の ちゅうがく 二ねんせい です。おんがく が すき です。ピアノ が とくい です。ひま な とき ピアノ を ひきます。

ぼく の なまえ は いわさき たけとし です。こうべ に すんで います。 しょうがく 一 ねんせい です。 ひま な とき こうえん で いぬ と あそびます。いぬ が だいすき です。

二

わたし は いしだ ひさえ です。ひろしま に すんで います。わたし は こうこう 一ねんせい です。がっこう は おんがく の がっこう です。おんがく が だいすき です。ひま な とき ともだち の うち で CD を ききます。

ぼく は あまのひでたか です。 とうきょう の しんじゅく に すんで います。ちゅうがく 一ねんせい です。 ぼく は supootsu が すき です。やきゅう が とくい です。ひま な とき ともだち と こうてい で やきゅう を します。

三

四

単語 (たんご)

New words

あそこ ___	over there
あそびます ___	play, muck about
おみやげ ___	souvenir, present
おもしろい ___	fun, interesting
きょねん ___	last year
こうてい ___	school ground, oval
ここ ___	here
しょうかい (します) ___	introduce
しゅうまつ ___	weekend
すてきな	nice, lovely
せんしゅ ___	player, athlete
そこ ___	there
たいかい ___	contest
たいいくかん ___	gymnasium
だれ ___	who
とくい ___	I am good at...
とけい ___	clock, watch
ひきます ___	play stringed or keyboard musical instruments
へや ___	room

Katakana の 単語

earobikusu ___	aerobics
erekutoon ___	electric organ
ooru-sutaa ___	All Stars
gitaa ___	guitar
saafin ___	surfing
CD (shiidii) ___	CD
dansu ___	dance
chanpion ___	champion
T-shatsu (tii shatsu) ___	T-shirt
dizuniirando ___	Disneyland
Hawai ___	Hawaii
basuketto booru ___	basketball
famikon ___	home computer
piano ___	piano
rokku konsaato ___	rock music concert

Expressions

あのこ、だれ? ___	Who is that kid?
あら? ___	Oh?!
うそ ___	That's a lie! I don't believe it!
おげんき ですか。 ___	How are you?
かっこいい! ___	Cool! Far out!
すてき! ___	Gorgeous!
そうだ! ___	Oh, I know!
ちょうどいい ___	just right
…ですって ___	he/she says that...
ひまな とき ___	spare time, free time
ほんとうかなあ ___	I wonder if that's true.
やめて! ___	Cut it out! Stop that!

Schools and year levels

しょうがっこう ___	primary school
ちゅうがっこう ___	junior high school
こうとうがっこう ___ (こうこう)	senior high school
しょうがく ___	primary school
…ねんせい	year level
ちゅうがく ___	junior high
…ねんせい	school year level
こうこう ___	senior high
…ねんせい	school year level

せいかつ

3-21, Yukinoshita 1-chome,
Kamakura-shi, Kanagawa-ken,
15th September   Japan

Hi everyone,

I wasn't going to write until I got a letter from
one of you, but at that rate you'll never hear from
me again. Where have you all been? On holidays,
I suppose. It would be nice to hear something
occasionally, you know. A card, maybe?

Anyway, I just had to write to show you these
latest photos. I bet you can't guess who this is.

Don't even try — it's Mr Tanaka. Old Mr Tanaka,
that is, the one who lives in the house behind the
one I live in. You know, you saw a picture of the
inside last year.

Doesn't he look great? Guess how old — no, I'll
tell you. He's 78. He's going through this really
trendy phase. Well, here's a picture of him about
twenty years ago, I think.

He was working for this company and then
became a manager or a director or something.
He just looks really ordinary, doesn't he? But
now that he's old, he says that he doesn't have
to worry about what people think or say any
more. He can just do his own thing. Everyone
looks up to old people here, and old Mr Tanaka
is really taking advantage of it. If he does something a bit weird, they all say, 'That's OK, he's
78.' Talk about old people's liberation!

I'd better tell you where he is in the first photo.
Well, the other day I noticed on the front seat
of his car, and in the glove box, all these
chocolate bars and sweets, so I asked him where
he got them all. He said, 'Come with me,' and
he took me to this huge, noisy, smoky place with
all these sort of pinball machines. It's called a
pachinko parlour. You could hear the music
blaring out from it from about ten blocks away,
no exaggeration. Pachinko parlours are really
popular in Japan. Really popular!!! He told me
to look as old as I could, because I don't think
I'm supposed to be in there until I'm 18.

You have to try to get as many of these little
metal balls out of the machines as you can, and
then you go and cash them in. Except you don't
get cash, you get cigarettes and sweets and things
like that. Well, old Mr Tanaka has heaps of these
things, which is funny, because he never eats
them and he doesn't smoke. When he asked me
what flavour sweets I wanted I said sutoroberii
(you know what I mean, don't you?). Well, I'll
never say that again. Old Mr Tanaka got really
cross and started going on about all these new
words coming in from English and taking over
from proper Japanese words. 'What's wrong
with いちご?' he kept asking. (That's the real
word for 'strawberry'.) It's just that when you
go to McDonald's or somewhere and ask for an
いちご sheeku they'll probably say, 'You
mean sutoroberii.' That's what happened when
I asked for さくらんぼ and was told that it was
cherii. I can see Mr Tanaka's point, really. It's
not like he's really old-fashioned. He just wants
to stop Japanese becoming full of these English-
sounding words.

You should have heard him when Toshio brought him back a terehon kaado as おみやげ from his trip over the Seto Bridge. You need these telephone cards for most public phones in the cities now, and the ones with pictures on the back are popular as souvenirs and presents — especially the really cute ones. Well, Mr Tanaka liked the present, but hated the word terehon. He didn't mind kaado so much, but he said terehon was stupid, and much harder to say than でんわ.

Don't get the idea that Mr Tanaka is always grumbling. He's not. He's really happy. He keeps busy going back to visit the factory where he was the boss and taking an interest in how it's going. He says most Japanese people are a bit scared of retirement. He says it's important to keep working at something.

Well, anyway, his factory makes these dolls and he took me to see them being made. I'll never forget the women who sat there putting the finishing touches to the dolls.

All they had to do was paint in the eyes and mouth. They were just so quick and accurate, and they could look up and talk to Mr Tanaka without making a mistake. Mr Tanaka is really proud of these dolls. He said that really important people from other countries take them home as souvenirs of Japan. They'd make great おみやげ, I think. He said Prince Charles took one home. I bet he gave it to Princess Di.

Guess what!! Well, this is tomorrow, and Mr Tanaka has just given me a ticket for the big Madonna concert in とうきょう tonight. What a present! They cost about eighty or ninety dollars here, you know. Someone at his factory gave it to him. The only thing is, when I thanked him for the きっぷ for the konsaato he said that it wasn't a きっぷ but a chiketto. I knew that, but I was trying to keep old Mr Tanaka happy. You can't win. Anyway I bought him a terehon kaado with Madonna on it and told him to use it for his でんわ calls.

Must dash now. I've got a konsaato to get ready for. And you probably need to get on with some homework. I'm rapt in Madonna. She's so sensitive and the words of her songs just mean so much.

Lots of love,

Simone.

P.S. NOTE!!! My address is at the top of the letter...just in case you've lost it!

日本語 ノート

一 Complimenting and bragging

When you compliment someone, or they praise you, じょうず is used. This means 'You're good at...' To accept a compliment, because you are modest, it is usual to say 'いいえ、そう でもない です' which means 'No, not really.'

When you are talking to someone about your abilities, you must use とくい to mean 'I'm good at...'

e.g. ぼく は supootsu が とくい です。

However, as in English, you shouldn't brag too much.

二 Saying where you live

To ask someone where they live and to tell them where you live, you say,

どこ に すんで いますか。
Where do you live?
よこはま に すんで います。
I live in Yokohama.

When you talk about where you live and use すんで います, the place is followed by に.

三 Talking about your school year level
なんねんせい ですか。

In Japan, it is very common to ask students what year level they are. Sometimes people ask this instead of なんさい ですか。
To say which year level student you are, you say しょうがく or ちゅうがく or こうこう for the kind of school and then add your year level and ねんせい. To say that you were in third year of junior high, you would say ちゅうがく 三ねんせい です。

The words for primary school, junior high school and senior high school all end in がっこう, although a senior high school is usually called こうこう. This is an abbreviation of こうとうがっこう. But when you talk about your year level, you change しょうがっこう and ちゅうがっこう to しょうがく and ちゅうがく before adding ねんせい.

四 Saying where you do things — at/in a place

To say that you do something *at* a place, you say で after the place. Sometimes in English we say *in* a place (e.g. in the library, in the school ground). This is also で.

e.g. あした ともだち の うち で terebi を みます。
Tomorrow I'm going to watch TV at my friend's house.
どこ で かいましたか。
Where did you buy it?
Hawai で かいました。
I bought it in Hawaii.

五 Saying where you do things — here, there, over there

The words ここ, そこ, あそこ correspond to *here* or *this place*, *there* or *that place* and *over there*. When you use あそこ, you would usually point to the place as it is away, from both you and the person you are talking to.

e.g. ここ に きて ください。
Come here.
そこ で たべましょう。
Let's eat at that place.
あそこ で ともだち に あいました。
I met my friend over there.

六 Playing

In Japanese there are many words for 'play'. When you play (or do) a sport or game, you say します.

e.g. Badominton を します。

When you play a stringed or keyboard musical instrument, you usually say ひきます.

e.g. Piano を ひきます。

But if you just hang about with your friends or play around with the dog, you use あそびます.

e.g. いぬ と あそびます。

七 More about adjectives

In きもの Level 1, you learnt to comment on things using adjectives.

e.g. かわいい ですね。

You can also put adjectives before a noun or a word you want to describe, as you do in English. You have done this with:

e.g. いいおてんき ですね。
It's a nice day, isn't it?

Here are some more examples:

あたらしい ともだち を
しょうかい します。
I'd like to introduce a new friend.
おもしろい おみやげ ですね。
What an interesting present!

八 ...ちゃん

...ちゃん is another form of address like ...さん and ...くん. But unlike ...さん and ...くん, ...ちゃん is never attached to a surname, only to a personal name or nickname. It is used to address small children and is also used by relatives and friends to address older girls.

がんばれ

Writing ひらがな

So, by now you have impressed all of your family and friends with your fantastic Japanese writing. But, deep down, you know that you still have some way to go before you can be fully satisfied with your ひらがな. Sometimes you look at a funny shape you have produced and realise that you have used an incorrect stroke order. At other times you realise that things are out of balance because the length of the strokes is not quite right.

But don't despair! Of course you need to keep working on your ひらがな! After all, your beautiful English handwriting was not something you mastered in just one year. Actually, Japanese children keep special 'doriru' books to practise their writing in. That's not a bad idea, is it?

Whether you choose to do that or not, you will need to make improving your ひらがな one of the goals for your second level of Japanese study. In the end, you will know that you have acquired a really special skill.

おめでとう!

You are now able to use your 日本語 to:

· introduce yourself
· ask where someone lives
· tell someone where you live
· find out what year level someone is in at school
· say what year level you are
· ask what someone does in their spare time
· ask and tell people where activities happen
· give and accept compliments

第二課・Maikuくん は どこ?

Puru-puru puru-puru puru-...

もしもし。

もしもし、みねさんの おたくですか。

はい、そうです。

あ、おばさん、Amandaです。こんにちは。

ああ、Amandaさん、こんにちは。おげんき ですか。

ええ、ありがとう ございます。あのう、ゆうこさん か はなこさん おねがい します。

はい、ちょっと まって... ゆうちゃん、でんわ! Amandaさん ですよ。

はあい!

もしもし ...

あ、ゆうこさん、いま なに を していましたか。

いや な しゅくだい...

ねえ、うみに いきませんか。

ええ...そう ですねえ...きょう は ちょっと...いま はなちゃん は あたらしい ともだち と あそんで います。

えっ?
あたらしい
ともだち?
だれですか。

さあ?
だれでしょうか。
あててみて。

ええと...せが たかい ですか。

いいえ、そんなに
たかくない です。でも、
あしが ながい ですよ。

へええ! めが
おおきい ですか。

ええ、おおきいです。
そして、きれいです。
みみも おおきいです。

ああそう...
hansamu
ですか。

ええ、とっても!とても
すてき です。いま booru
あそび を しています。

ねえ、Amandaさん、
いま うちに
きませんか。

第二課 ● 十五

ええ！ すぐ いきます！
じゃあね。 Bai bai。

Bai bai。

Maikuくん、Maikuくん...

峰 (みね)

KOTSU KOTSU

はあい！ あ、Amandaさん、
どうぞ あがって。

どこ？ どこ？
Maikuくん は
どこ？

えっ？ Maiku？ この いぬ の
なまえ は Chappii ですよ。

Chappii, おいで！

いいましょう 一

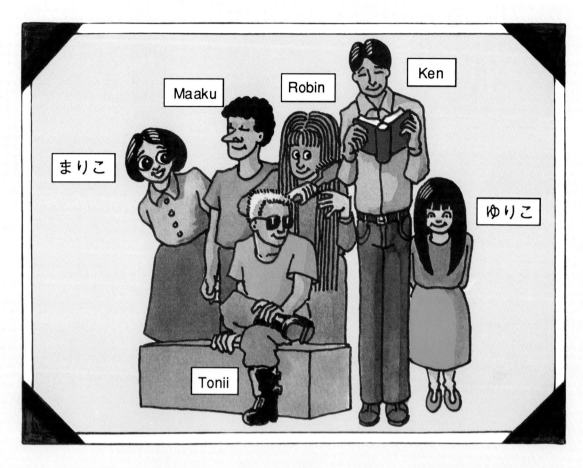

Using the example as a guide, comment on the people in the drawing.
The expressions given in the box may be of use.

例:

> A この ひと は せ が たかい ですね。
> だれ ですか。
> B Kenくん です。

めが おおきい
せが たかい
せが ひくい
かみ が ながい
かみ が みじかい

おかあさん は せが ひくい
ですね。じゅんいちくん は
せが たかい ですね。

いいましょう 二

一 hansamu な ひと
ゆうめい な ひと
いや な ひと

二 きれい な ひと
しずか な ひと
ゆうめい な ひと

三 へん な ひと
いや な ひと
すてき な ひと

第二課 ● 十八

①

②

③

④

⑤

Using the examples as a guide, comment on the pictures.

例:

A hansamu な ひと です ね。
B そう です ね。
　　or
　　そう です か。

例:

A この ひと は hansamu です ね。
B そう です ね。
　　or
　　そう です か。

いいましょう 三

かお を
あらって
います。

すうがく を
べんきょう
して います。

でんしゃ を
まって
います。

本 を
よんで
います。

まんが を
かいて
います。

一

二

三

四

五

六

Look at the pictures and ask your partner what each person is doing.

例:

A この ひと は いま なに を して (い)ますか。
B かお を あらって (い)ます。

第二課 ● 十九

Invite someone to share in these activities.
They may accept or decline.

例:

A きょう じょうば に いきませんか。
B ええ、いい ですね。
　or
　じょうば ですか。じょうば は ちょっと...

You may suggest another activity.

例:

A きょう じょうば に いきませんか。
B じょうば ですか。じょうば は ちょっと...
A じゃ、saikuringu は?
B ええ、いい ですよ。

You may arrange a better time.

例:

A きょう じょうば に いきませんか。
B きょう は ちょっと...
A じゃ、あしたは?
B あした ですか。ええ、いい ですよ。

ともだちと

Make up a conversation with a partner.
Decide who will be A and who will be B.

A | [B] さん、[B] くん、 | なに を して いますか。

B | しゃしん を みて います。

A | しゃしん ですか。みせて ください。

B | どうぞ。

A | あっ、ねこ の しゃしん ですね。とても | へんな きれいな おもしろい | ねこ ですね。

| みみ が ながい めが おおきい あし が みじかい | ですね。この ねこ は なに を して いますか。 |

B | あ、Buronson は | terebi を みて います。 CD を きいて います。 booru あそび を して います。 | terebi booru あそび おんがく | が だいすき です。

| ねえ、 | [A] さん、[A] くん、 | あした | あたらしい CD を ききませんか。 basuketto booru を しませんか。 うみ に いきませんか。 bideo を みませんか。 |

A | あした は ちょっと...

B | じゃ、らいしゅう の | どようび にちようび | は?

A | どようび にちようび | ですか。いい ですよ。

いってみましょう

There are several ways of making telephone calls. Here are two patterns.

たけしくん is ringing the やまだ house to talk to his friend,
たろうくん. Mr やまだ answers the phone.

1 やまださん:　もしもし。
　 たけし:　　　もしもし。やまださん の おたく ですか。
　 やまださん:　はい、そう です。
　 たけし:　　　たけし です。あのう、たろうくん おねがい
　　　　　　　　します。
　 やまださん:　はい、ちょっと まってください。

2 たろう:　　　もしもし。やまだ です。
　 たけし:　　　ああ、たろうくん。たけし です。

At the end of your call, you can say じゃあね, an informal way of saying
'goodbye' which should be used only with people you know well.

Now it's your turn. Ring up a friend. His or her mother answers the
phone so you have to ask for your friend. Invite your friend to go
somewhere or to participate in an activity with you. This friend is not
keen on what you suggest so arrange to go somewhere else. Also, the
time you suggest is inconvenient for your friend so try to arrange a time
to suit you both. You will need to arrange where and at what time you
will meet and then ring off.

せいかつ

A letter from Simone.

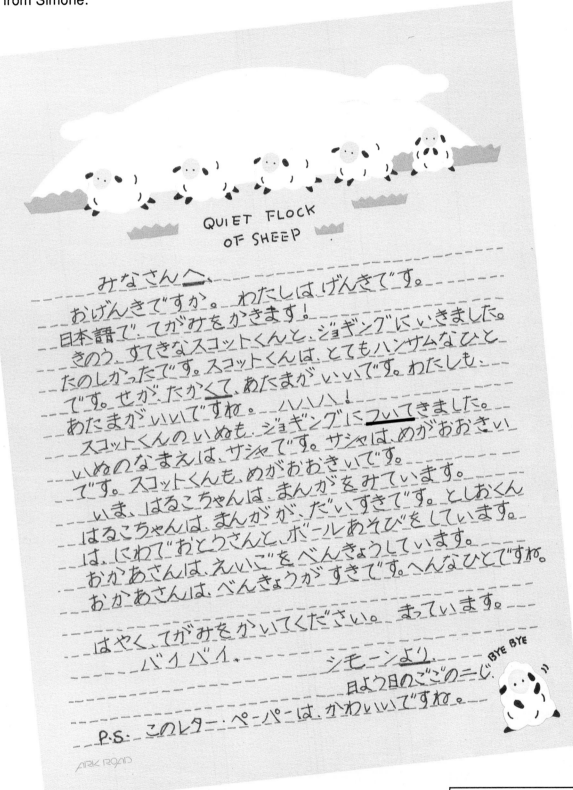

QUIET FLOCK
OF SHEEP

みなさん へ、
おげんきですか。わたしは げんきです。
日本語で、てがみを かきます!
きのう、すてきな スコットくんと、ジョギングに いきました。
たのしかったです。スコットくんは、とても ハンサムな ひと
です。せが たかくて、あたまが いいです。わたしも、
あたまが いいですね。ハハハ!
スコットくんの いぬも、ジョギングに ついてきました。
いぬの なまえは、サシャです。サシャは、めが おおきい
です。スコットくんも、めが おおきいです。
いま、はるこちゃんは まんがを みています。
はるこちゃんは まんがが、だいすきです。としおくん
は、にわで おとうさんと、ボールあそびを しています。
おかあさんは、えいごを べんきょう しています。
おかあさんは、べんきょうが すきです。へんな ひとですね。
はやく、てがみを かいてください。まっています。
バイバイ。
                    シモーンより
                    日よう日の ごごの 二じ。 BYE BYE
このレター・ペーパーは、かわいいですね。

P.S.

ARK ROAD

へ	to
たかくて	tall <u>and</u>
ついて	follow
より	from

日本語 ノート

一 Describing yourself and others

In きもの 1, when you learnt to say who likes something, you said

> はなこさん は おかし が すき です。
> Hanako likes sweets.

You can use this same pattern to describe how someone looks.

e.g. Terii くん は せが たかい です。
Terry is tall.
Chappii ちゃん は あし が ながい です。
Chappy has long legs.
Dambo は みみ が おおきいです。
Dumbo has big ears.

This pattern is also used to describe how intelligent someone is.

e.g. Amanda さん は あたま が いい です。
Amanda is clever.

二 More about describing

You know lots of good words to describe things.

e.g. つまらない　　むずかしい
ちいさい　　　あたらしい

All of these adjectives end with い, so we call them い adjectives. There is another group of adjectives that doesn't end in い (e.g. いや, しずか) – these are called な adjectives because when they are followed directly by a noun , な has to be included.

e.g. いやな しゃしん ですね。
What a horrible photo!

If you are not using a noun directly after the adjective, then な is not used.

e.g. この しゃしん は いや ですね。
This photo is horrible, isn't it?

There are some exceptions to the rule about い adjectives: even though きれい and ゆうめい end in い, they are な adjectives. You must put な after them when a noun follows directly.

e.g. きれい な きもの ですね。
Isn't that a pretty kimono.

ゆうめい な みせで かいました。
She bought it at a famous shop.

三 Agreeing and disagreeing

Note that when you say そう ですね, you are agreeing with your friend's comment.
If you don't really agree, you can say そう ですか with a rising tone.

四 Inviting people out

When you want to invite people to do things or go to places, you use the ...ませんか ending on verbs. In 日本語 you are really asking 'Won't you ...?' Of course, in English we usually say 'Would you like to...'

e.g. きょう かいもの に いきませんか。
Would you like to go shopping today?

If you really enjoy shopping, you'd accept the invitation by saying,

> ええ、いい ですね。
> Yeah, that'd be good.

If you are not that keen on shopping, you could say,

> かいもの ですか。かいもの は ちょっと...
> Shopping? I don't really like shopping...

and when your friend suggests something better, you can then accept by saying,

> ええ、いい ですよ。
> Yes, that sounds good.

If you'd like to go, but can't go today, you say,

> きょう は ちょっと...
> Today is not very good for me...

You can then work out a more suitable time. Note that sometimes a question repeating the activity or time is used.

e.g. A あした じょうば に いきませんか。
B じょうば ですか。じょうば は ちょっと...

This is to confirm what you heard, or you may use it just to give you some extra time to think.

五 て form of verbs

You have already met many examples of verbs in て form.

e.g. かして、すわって、きいて

Think of て as a base form of the verb. When you add words to the base form you get other meanings. If you add ください, it becomes a request.

e.g. けし gomu を かして ください。
ここ に きて ください。

If you add います to the て form, it tells you what someone is doing now.

e.g. たけしくん は いま なに を して いますか。
What is Takeshi doing?
Terebi を みて います。
He's watching TV.

When you hear Japanese people speaking, you'll hear that they shorten て います to て ます。

e.g. 日本語 を べんきょう して (い)ます。
I'm studying Japanese.
本 を よんで (い)ます。
He's reading a book.

Because て form is a base form, you need to know how to form it. This chart of verbs, which you already know, shows that how you form the て base form depends on what kind of verb you are dealing with and what comes before ます。

You will notice that a couple of groups end in で instead of て but we still call this the て form. The て form is a complex form and you probably will find it difficult at first. But, like most things in 日本語, it looks harder than it really is!

ーます form	て form
WEAK	
あけます	あけて
しめます	しめて
たべます	たべて
みせます	みせて
みます	みて
STRONG	
すわります	すわって
あいます	あって
あらいます	あらって
いいます	いって
かいます	かって
たちます	たって
まちます	まって
かきます	かいて
ききます	きいて
ひきます	ひいて
あそびます	あそんで
のみます	のんで
よみます	よんで
かします	かして
IRREGULAR	
いきます	いって
きます	きて
します	して

おめでとう！

You are now able to use your 日本語 to:

· describe people and things
· invite friends out
· accept and decline an invitation
· say what people are doing at this moment
· get a friend to the phone when you ring

単語 (たんご)

New words
い adjectives

たかい ___ high, expensive
ながい ___ long
ひくい ___ low
みじかい ___ short

Expressions

あててみて ___ have a guess
ありがとう ございます ___ thank you very much
おいで ___ come here (calling a dog)
おねがい します ___ may I have...?
そん なに (たかくない) ___ not that (tall)
だれ でしょうか ___ who do you think?

な adjectives

いや ___ horrible, terrible
きれい ___ pretty, clean
しずか ___ quiet
すてき ___ nice, wonderful
hansamu ___ good-looking, handsome
へん ___ strange
ゆうめい ___ famous

え ___ picture, painting
おたく ___ your house
か ___ or
かきます ___ write, draw
この ひと ___ this person, he/she
しゃしん ___ photograph
しんぶん ___ newspaper
とても ___ very
とっても ___ very!
べんきょう します ___ study
ひと ___ person
booru あそび ___ playing with a ball

Parts of the body

かみ (のけ) hair
せ height
め eyes
あたま head
はな nose
みみ ears
かお face
ゆび fingers
くち mouth
て hands
からだ body
あし legs, feet
あしのゆび toes

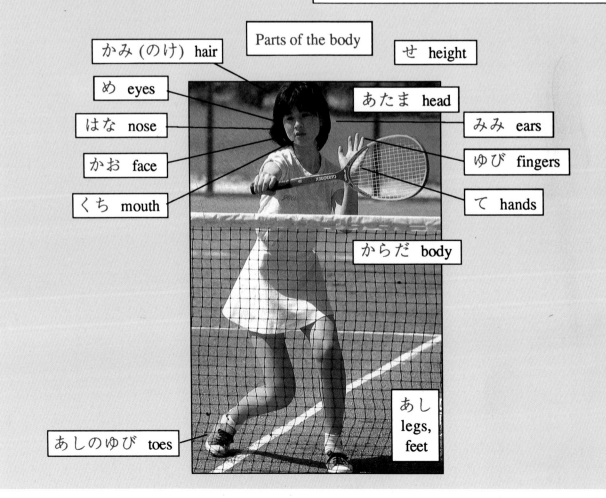

カタカナ

As you know, ordinary written Japanese uses a mixture of *hiragana*, *kanji* and *katakana*.

Katakana is used mainly for words and names borrowed from other languages. Since most *katakana* words are derived from English, they are easy to understand, e.g. tenisu (テニス), basu (バス), hotto doggu (ホット ドッグ). However, there are many borrowed words which have been shortened or changed so that they no longer seem like English words, e.g. famikon (ファミコン).

Katakana is used for some Japanese words. These include noise words (e.g. wan wan ワン ワン for a dog's bark), baby talk, slang, technical words, company names and nicknames. *Katakana* is also sometimes used in the same way as we use *italics*, to make something stand out visually. Below is the katakana chart.

	A	I	U	E	O
	ア	イ	ウ	エ	オ
K	カ	キ	ク	ケ	コ
G	ガ	ギ	グ	ゲ	ゴ
S	サ	シ	ス	セ	ソ
Z	ザ	ジ	ズ	ゼ	ゾ
T	タ	チ	ツ	テ	ト
D	ダ	(ヂ) (ji)	(ヅ) (zu)	デ	ド
N	ナ	ニ	ヌ	ネ	ノ
H	ハ	ヒ	フ	ヘ	ホ
B	バ	ビ	ブ	ベ	ボ
P	パ	ピ	プ	ペ	ポ
M	マ	ミ	ム	メ	モ
Y	ヤ		ユ		ヨ
R	ラ	リ	ル	レ	ロ
W	ワ				ヲ (o)
N	ン (n)				

Look closely at the カタカナ chart. The most obvious difference between カタカナ and ひらがな is that the カタカナ letters have sharp angles and straighter lines. Although this makes the letters easier to write, it does not lessen the task of learning them all! You probably had some good ways for learning ひらがな. You can use many of these to help you remember カタカナ. Here are some further hints:

・ There are several カタカナ that look like their ひらがな equivalent, e.g. カ (か), キ (き) and ヘ (へ). ニ look like かんじ 二.

・ As you did with ひらがな, see if you can see a picture in each letter that will help you remember the sound. Can you see ro (ロ), for robotto (ロボット) in the illustration below?

・ There are some groups of similar-looking カタカナ, e.g. ツ tsu, ソ so, ノ no. One way to remember these is to make up some reminders. For example, you could say that tsu (ツ) has tsu (two) small strokes, no (ノ) has no small strokes and so (ソ) is the sole letter with one stroke.

Unfortunately there are no short-cuts to learning カタカナ. As you discovered when you learnt ひらがな, what is really necessary is some hard work! However, once you have learnt to read カタカナ you will be able to expand your vocabulary very quickly as most カタカナ words are easy to remember. Many signs and menus in Japan are written in カタカナ and when you visit Japan, you'll be surprised at how much you can read.

Writing カタカナ

You will be doing lots of writing practice in your *Workbook* but first let's look at the similarities and differences between spelling rules in カタカナ and in ひらがな.

Little tsu ッ

Just as in ひらがな when little つ is used to double the sound of the consonant that follows (e.g. すわって), little ッ in カタカナ does the same.

e.g.　ペット　　petto
　　　キッス　　kissu
　　　トラック　torakku

Little ya ャ , yu ュ , yo ョ

Little ャ, ョ, ュ combine in the same way as they did in ひらがな to make a new sound.

	ヤ	ユ	ヨ
キ	キャ	キュ	キョ
ギ	ギャ	ギュ	ギョ
シ	シャ	シュ	ショ
ジ	ジャ	ジュ	ジョ
チ	チャ	チュ	チョ
ニ	ニャ	ニュ	ニョ
ヒ	ヒャ	ヒュ	ヒョ
ビ	ビャ	ビュ	ビョ
ピ	ピャ	ピュ	ピョ
ミ	ミャ	ミュ	ミョ
リ	リャ	リュ	リョ

Examples of words using these sounds are:

T シャツ　　T-shatsu
ジュニア　　junia
ジョギング　jogingu

Making double vowel sounds

In ひらがな, as you know, there are two ways of making double vowel sounds. One is to repeat the vowel as in おかあさん and おにいさん and おねえさん. The other rule is for double お sounds when the double お is written with う as in おとうさん and おはよう.

When writing in カタカナ, this double vowel sound is written as a bar.

e.g.　スポーツ　supootsu
　　　ギター　　gitaa
　　　ニュース　nyuusu
　　　ケーキ　　keeki

When writing vertically, the bar becomes vertical too.

e.g.　ケーキ　ニュース　ギター　スポーツ

Making new sounds

There are some sound combinations that have been created just to write foreign words. Sounds like *fa*, *fi*, *che*, *di* are sounds that do not exist in Japanese words. These new sounds are written using little ア, イ, エ, オ and ユ. (See below.)

ア	クァ kwa	グァ gwa				ツァ tsa			ファ fa
イ							ティ ti	ディ di	フィ fi
エ		シェ she	ジェ je	チェ che	ツェ tse				フェ fe
オ	クォ kwo					ツォ tso			フォ fo
ユ								デュ dyu	

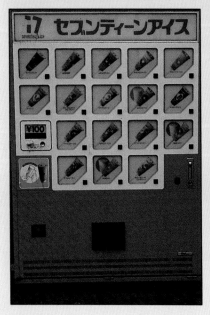

第三課・へん じゃない ですよ。

げつようび

ゆうこさん、もう うち に かえりますか。

ええ。

あっ... はなこさん は びょうき です ね。

ねえ、おみまい に いきません か。

ええ、いきましょう。

いい です か。

ええ、どうぞ きて ください。

ただいま。

おかえり なさい。あら、みなさん...

おじゃま します。

どうぞ。 どうぞ。

あっ? マスク!? へん です ねえ。

はなちゃん、どう?

へん じゃない です よ。いま かぜ を ひいて います。

みんな！あたらしい
ファミコンゲーム を
しませんか。さあ、
ホセくん、ここ に
すわって...

ええと... イタリア では
なに語 を はなしますか。

イタリア語 を
はなします。

まる！じゃ、
つぎ！

ジアングくん、
フランス では
なに語 を
はなしますか。

フランス語 を
はなします。

まる！

アメリカ では？

えい語 を はなします。
ゴホン、ゴホン...

まる！どうしたん ですか。

のど が いたいん です。

すみません、ぼく... うち に
かえります。おじゃま しました。

じゃ つぎ... アマンダさん...

カナダ で なに語
を はなしますか。

えい語。

フランス語。

はい、そう です。よく
できました。まる! あら?
アマンダさん、どうしたん
ですか。

じゃ、ジアングくん、
メキシコ...

メキシコ語...

だめ! ばつ!
メキシコ人 は
スペイン語 を
はなします。
ジアングくん
はだめ!
じゃつぎ!

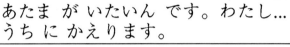

あたま が いたいん です。わたし...
うち に かえります。

はなちゃん、ここ に きて。

だめ ですよ。わたし は
かぜを ひいて います。

つぎ は ぼく...

かようび

あら... みなさん... しずか
ですね。どうしたんですか。

かぜ を ひいて います!

すいようび

せんせい、どうしたん
ですか。しずか ですね。

第三課 ● 三十三

いいましょう 一

Using the pictures as a guide, talk about what is wrong with you.

例:

A どうしたん ですか。
B おなか が いたいん です。

いいましょう 二

Using the example as a guide, talk about where the scouts and guides are from.

例:

> A ひでおくん は どこ から きましたか。
> B 日本 から きました。

Using the example as a guide, talk about what language (or languages) the scouts and guides speak.

例:

> A ひでおくん は なに語 を はなしますか。
> B 日本語 と えい語 を はなします。

Using the example as a guide, talk about the nationalities of the scouts and guides.

例:

> A ひでおくん は ちゅうごく人 ですか。
> B いいえ、日本人 です。

いいましょう 三

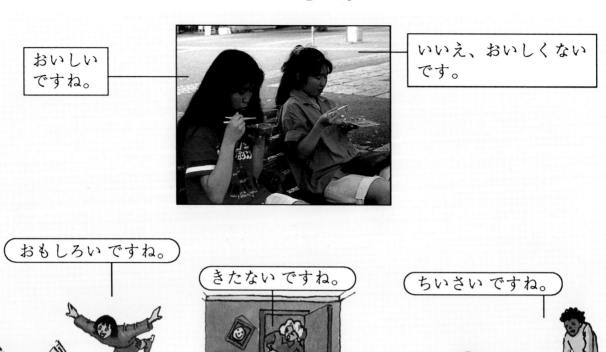

おいしい
ですね。

いいえ、おいしくない
です。

おもしろい ですね。

一

きたない ですね。

三

ちいさい ですね。

五

むずかしい ですね。

二

おいしい ですね。

四

あつい ですね。

六

第三課 ● 三十六

Listen to the example below, look at the pictures and respond
with what you imagine the other person is saying.

例:

A おもしろい ですね。
B いいえ、おもしろくない です。

しずか ですね。

しずか ですね。

一

いや ですね。

二

きれい ですね。

三

へん ですね。

四

ゆうめい ですね。

五

Listen to the example below, look at the pictures and respond
with what you imagine the other person is saying.

例:

A しずか ですね。
B いいえ、しずか じゃない です。

てんき

きょうの てんき

あしたの てんき

☀	fine	はれ でしょう		it will be fine
☁	cloudy	くもり でしょう		it will be cloudy
🌧	rain	あめ でしょう		it will rain
❄❄	snow	ゆき でしょう		it will snow
⛅	fine/cloudy	はれ のち くもり でしょう		it will be fine; cloudy later
🌦	cloudy/rain	くもり のち あめ でしょう		it will be cloudy; rain later
🌧☀	rain/fine	あめ のち はれ でしょう		it will rain; fine later
❄☀	snow/fine	ゆき のち はれ でしょう		it will snow; fine later

Talk about the weather today and tomorrow in the city of your choice.

A とうきょう の てんき は どう ですか。
B はれ です。
A 何ど ですか。
B 5ど です。
A あした は どう でしょうか。
B あめ でしょう。

てんき − weather　でしょう − it will be　のち − later　ど − degrees

ともだちと

Make up a conversation with a partner.
Decide who will be A and who will be B.

がっこう で

A	[B]さん、 [B]くん、	ひろしくん ミシェルさん マリオくん アンさん	は	らいしゅう	日本 フランス イタリア イギリス	に かえりますね。

きょう あした どようび に	おみやげを かいましょうか。

B	ええ、そう しましょう。

デパート で

B	あっ、この	おんがく ビデオ とけい 本	を	きいて みて	ください。	おもしろい いい きれい すてき	ですね。

A	えっ? そう ですか。	おもしろくない よくない きれいじゃない すてきじゃない	ですよ。

とても	うるさい へんな つまらない	おんがく ビデオ とけい 本	です。これ は どう ですか。

B	それ は ちょっと...。	ひろしくん ミシェルさん マリオくん アンさん	は	ファミコンを しますか。 まんがを よみますか。 えを かきますか。 テニスを しますか。

A	ええ、	します。 よみます。 かきます。

第三課 ● 三十九

| B | じゃ、 | ファミコン ゲーム
まんが
かみ と クレヨン
テニス の 本 | を かいましょうか。 |

| A | あ、それ は いい ですね。 |

いってみましょう

いいえ...

You have a friend who is great company but is really lazy. No matter what you suggest doing, this friend always has an excuse for not going along with you.

You have to come up with as many suggestions or invitations as possible about where to go and what to do. Try to persuade your friend by telling him or her that it will be fun or easy. Your classmate, who is role-playing your friend, has to think up as many excuses as possible for not going to these places or for not doing these things.

Here are some examples to get you going.

Suggestion/invitation	Excuse
サイクリング に いきませんか。 ハンバーガー を たべましょうか。 サッカー を しましょうか。 ボール あそび を しませんか。	サイクリング は ちょっと... ハンバーガー は あんまり... あし が いたいん です。 ボール あそび は おもしろくない です。

You know you have won the day when your friend runs out of excuses.

ローラー スケート を しませんか。

日本語 ノート

 一 It hurts...!

The Japanese word for *ouch!* or *it hurts!* is いたい. When you want to explain what part of your body is sore, you use the following expression:

...が いたいん です。

So, if a headache is the reason you can't do the test scheduled for today, you'd look pained and say,

あたま が いたいん です。

If you have a sore throat, you can suffer in silence or say,

のど が いたいん です。

To find out what the matter with someone is, you ask,

どうしたん ですか。

二 Coming and going

When you invite someone to come to your house, you use the verb きます (*come*), but when they accept, they use いきます (*go*).

e.g. ようこさん、ぼく のうち に
きませんか。
Yoko, will you come to my place?
ええ、いきます。
Yes, I'll come.

You could say that ええ、いきます means *Yes, I'll go (to your house).*

いきます is always used when you go somewhere else. When you talk about someone coming to where you are, you must use きます.

Another use of きます is found in the expression どこからきましたか。This means *Where do you come from?* and is used to ask someone's country of birth.

三 Returning home

When you ask someone when they are going home, you use the verb かえります (*go home, return*).

e.g. いつ うち に かえりますか。
When are you going home?

If someone is going back to their country, they will also use かえります. Someone who lives in アメリカ might tell you,

らいげつ アメリカ に かえります。
I'm going back to America next month.

四 Some more set expressions

By now, you've probably realized that Japanese has many set expressions that you are required to use in given situations. When you are a visitor to a friend's house, you say おじゃま します as you enter. When you leave, you say おじゃ ましました. While this expression means *I'm in your way*, you can think of it as meaning *Thank you for having me.*

There are also expressions and responses that are used when people leave their own house and when they arrive back home. You probably remember these from きもの 1.

いってきます。 いってらっしゃい。

ただいま。 おかえりなさい。

五 It's not difficult! It's not strange!

You already know that when you want to say that something is difficult, you say むずかしい です. If you want to say that it is not difficult, you say むずかしくない です.

Another example is,

おおきい ですね。　It's big, isn't it?
おおきくない です。　It isn't big.

The only exception to this pattern for い adjectives is いい, which doesn't have a negative form. Fortunately there is another word, よい, which means *good* or *nice* and it does have a negative form, よくない. So, you might hear people disagreeing by saying,

いい ですね。
That's good, isn't it?
よくない です。
It's not good.

If you want to say that something (or someone) is strange, you say へん です. If you want to say that it is not strange, you say,

へんじゃない です

Another example is,

きれい ですね。
It's pretty, isn't it?
きれい じゃない です。
It's not pretty.

There are no exceptions to this pattern for **な** adjectives.

単語 (たんご)

	Country	Nationality -人	Language -語
	日本	日本人	日本語
	ちゅうごく	ちゅうごく人	ちゅうごく語
	アメリカ	アメリカ人	えい語
	イギリス	イギリス人	えい語
	イタリア	イタリア人	イタリア語
	インドネシア	インドネシア人	インドネシア語
	オーストラリア	オーストラリア人	えい語
	カナダ	カナダ人	えい語、フランス語
	ニュージーランド	ニュージーランド人	えい語
	ドイツ	ドイツ人	ドイツ語
	フランス	フランス人	フランス語
	メキシコ	メキシコ人	スペイン語

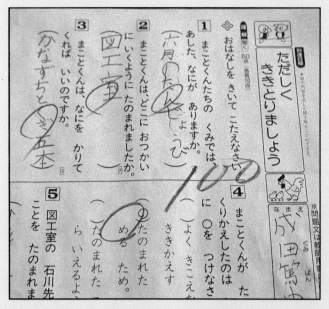

Imagine that you have received this piece of corrected work back from your teacher. You might be anxious about the red circles called まる. Perhaps you would be reassured by the 100 and the teacher's comment of よく できました *Well done!* In Japan, まる represents correct work like a tick, whereas ばつ means wrong or incorrect. ばつ is written as X.

New words and expressions

かえります —	return, go home
はなします —	speak
もう —	already

おみまい Visiting someone who is sick

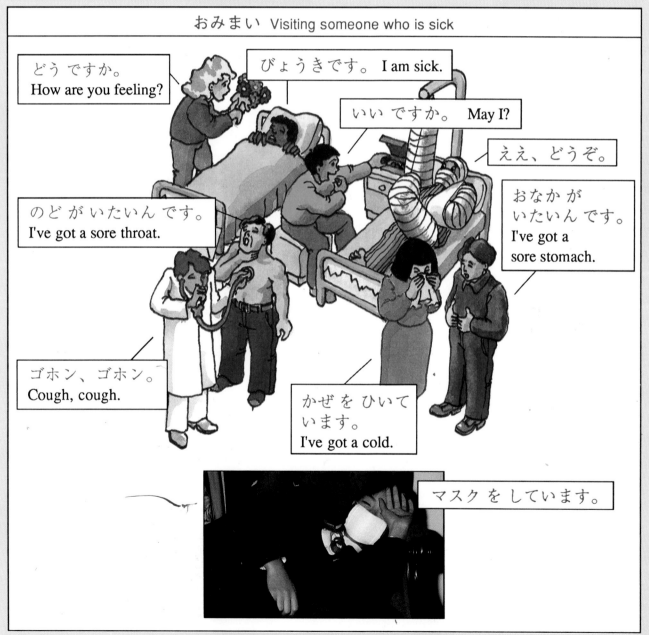

せいかつ

Meet ゆきこ and えつこ, two young office ladies with the Mitsubishi Bank in とうきょう. They both started working there at the beginning of last year and have become very good friends. Now they are nearing the end of their second year with the bank, and most of their lunchtime conversations are about one thing: their annual holidays. They plan to take them in just over a month's time.

ゆきこ and えつこ were still at university when Japanese workers only got two weeks' annual leave. Now nearly everyone gets three weeks and more and more young people plan to 'go away' for most of that time.

Fortunately, they earn very good wages and most young people like ゆきこ and えつこ find it fairly easy to save. Both of them still live at home so they don't have to worry about big living expenses like food and rent. えつこ was thinking of buying a car, but, as ゆきこ pointed out, she has nowhere at home to keep it and the traffic in and around the city makes driving far too difficult. So, all they have to spend their money on is clothes — expensive clothes, mind you, and always with designer labels. And ゆきこ, especially, spends quite a bit on music. She has the latest pop CDs from all over the world. But that still leaves quite a bit to spend on their holidays, and the Japanese government really encourages people to spend some of their savings.

So where to this year? Well, both of them have already been to Europe. えつこ was given a trip to London, Paris and Rome as a graduation present at the end of her university course. ゆきこ went there at the end of her first year with the bank. It was a group holiday organised by the bank, and she still has sixty-two group photos to prove it. And えつこ still has the perfume in the Eiffel Tower bottle that her friend brought back as おみやげ. So when they look at the Europe brochures and schedules, it's more a case of nostalgia than practical planning.

What about somewhere exotic, like Australia? And Hawaii looks かわいい. But every time えつこ suggests one of these places, ゆきこ tries to change the subject. Eventually she admits that she is reserving one of them for her honeymoon.

ハワイアン ウェディング

オーストラリア
ウェディング

シドニー

ゴールド コースト

What they need now is something new and exciting, a new experience. After all, they seem to lead highly organized lives. Even their leisure time seems full of discipline. ゆきこ has been going to tea ceremony classes for about 18 months now, and progress seems so slow. She enjoys it, but sometimes she feels she will never really master it. えつこ feels much the same way about her flower arranging class.

And so they reach a decision. They will go on one of the holiday packages in Japan offering to teach them a new skill in just a few days. So, what will it be? Horse riding? Tennis? Scuba diving?

ゆきこ doesn't mind which one it is, as long as it has おんせん. おんせん are hot springs and the natural hot water is piped into big baths. At the resort hotels おんせん baths often overlook the sea or a valley. Some are outdoors and ゆきこ went to one in winter where she soaked in an outdoor hot pool surrounded by snow. As ゆきこ says, a relaxing おんせん could be just what is needed after a day on horseback.

スクーバダイビング

イントロダクトリースペシャル			
日何		プレイ	ホテル
1	ANA ✈ ホテル 🚌	フリータイム	オーシャン ビューホテル
2	ダイビング・フリータイム	午前 a.m.: スクーバ・ダイビング1日1 ダイブ（タンク1本） 午後 p.m.: オプショナル・ダイビング	オーシャン ビューホテル
3	ホテル 🚕 ANA ✈	フリータイム	

テニススクール

アスレジャークラブ

🎾 レンタルテニス	♨ おんせん	⛳ ゴルフ
🚲 レンタルサイクル	👟 レジャーランド	🏊 プール

スケジュール		
1	JR - 11.30 🚌 13.00 - 17.00 20.00 - 21.00	ウエルカム ドリンク (コーヒー or ティー) レッスン VTR による ミーティング
2	9.00 - 12.00 13.00 - 17.00 19.00 - 21.00	レッスン レッスン パーティー
3	9.30 - 12.00 14.00 - 16.00 17.00	レッスン フリータイム JR 🚌

乗馬スクール
じょうば

ラングラー ランチ

マスター3 Days ・ スケジュール		
1	11.00 13.00 15.00	チェックイン 乗馬レッスン フリータイム (パターゴルフ を どうぞ)
2	10.00 11.00 14.30 16.00	ミーティング 乗馬レッスン 乗馬レッスン フリータイム (サウナ を どうぞ)
3	10.00 12.00	乗馬レッスン チェックアウト

がんばれ

Learning the words

One thing that should be clear to you by now is that attending classes is only part of what is required of you as a language learner. Just being 'there' is not enough! No matter how many lively activities you take part in, you still need to find some quiet learning times of your own so that you can master the new words and expressions that you are meeting. You sometimes hear people complain that they learn the たんご but forget everything the next day. That's because they don't know these helpful hints for vocabulary learning.

1 For every word that you are learning, make up a personal memory system that ensures that you won't forget it. The best way is to use sound and image association. Take the word きたない, for example. Don't just read it, say it out loud, and say it 'dirty'. That -ない ending on the word makes it easy to say it with a filthy, grimy feeling. Think 'dirty' while you say it: piles of greasy dishes or muddy sneakers on white carpet. The word きれい, on the other hand, is just right for saying in a light, 'pretty' way. You will never forget しずか if you concentrate on the first sound as you say it.

These memory aids may sound silly, but that's the whole point. The sillier your personal system is, the more likely it is that you will remember the words.

2 Don't just run your eye up and down the word lists a couple of times. Get busy with a pen and paper. Write words down (this will help your ひらがな writing too), especially the ones that you keep getting wrong. Test yourself by covering first one side of the たんご, then the other.

3 Divide and conquer. Set yourself realistic targets. Don't attempt to learn a whole page at a time, but take advantage of the fact that your きもの word lists are divided into convenient, manageable sections.

4 It takes two to たんご. Get someone else involved in your vocabulary learning. Ask a family member to 'hear' you. They probably won't know if you are wrong or right, but you will, and that's the most important thing. You can arrange to have a たんご partner at school — agree to test each other regularly.

Whatever method you choose, remember it's up to you. You can't just expect to absorb all the Japanese you need to know just by being there.

おめでとう

You are now able to use your 日本語 to:

- find out what is wrong with someone
- describe your aches and pains
- describe things and people
- talk about people's nationalities and what language they speak
- be a polite visitor
- read lots of country names in カタカナ
- talk about the weather

第四課 ・ チャッピー！こら！

チャッピーちゃん、
さんぽに いきましょう。
あら？ どう したんですか。

ゆうちゃん、チャッピー は いすの
したに います。びょうきかな？

びょうき？ほんとう？

おなか が すいて いますか。ほら、
ヤミー ですよ。たべて。あら？
たべませんね。へん ですね。

はなちゃん、びょういんに
でんわ を しましょう！

もしもし。
びょういん
ですか。

はい、そう です。

あのう...うちの
いぬ が びょうき
なんです。

ええと... いま は ちょっと...こんで いますよ。
いぬ が 五ひき います。ねこ が 三びき います。
そして へび が 六ぴき います。たくさん
まって います。あした きて ください。

でも... でも...
おねがいします。

つぎ!

つぎ は かめ です。

かめ は どこ?

ええと... いすの したに います。

チャッピー は びょうき... ヤミー を たべません。

じゃ... どうぞ 二じ に きて ください。

つぎ は?

その ねこ です。カーテン の うしろ に います。

この いぬ は びょうき じゃない ですよ。なまけもの です。ふとりすぎ です。じゃ...

ギャア!

ギャア! ギャア!

ワン、ワン!

ニャー、ニャー!

あーっ!

さる は どこ に いますか。

あっ! あそこ、あそこ!
きの うえ に います。

ぶた は... あっ!
ぶた は ベンチ の
うしろ に います。

ぶた は...?

とり は くるま の した に いますよ。

一ぴき、二ひき、三びき、四ひき...

はずかしかった。

だめ な チャッピー！

ただいま。

おねえちゃん、ぼく の チョコレート を たべましたか。

わたし じゃない ですよ。

としちゃんの チョコレート？ たべません でしたよ。

あっ！チャッピー！こら！

第四課 ● 五十

いいましょう 一

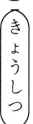
一 きょうしつ

二 みせ

こうてい
三

四 へや

五 たいいくかん

Using the examples as a guide, talk about where りえさん is.

例:

A りえさん は どこ に いますか。
B きょうしつ に います。

例:

A りえさん は どこ ですか。
B きょうしつ です。

いいましょう 二

Using the example below as a guide, talk about where the animals are.

例:

> A かめ は どこ に いますか。
> B いす の うえ に います。

Using the example below as a guide, ask ひろしくん about his pets.

例:

> A ペット を かって いますか。
> B はい、ねこ を 三びき かって います。

いぬ を 一ぴき
かって います。

いいましょう 三

一

コーヒー を のみます。

二

しんぶん を よみます。

三

しゅくだい を します。

四

ギター を ひきます。

五

テレビを みます。

六

てがみ を かきます。

Using the example as a guide, talk about these activities.

例:

A よく コーヒー を のみますか。
B いいえ、あまり のみません。

ともだちと

Make up a conversation with a partner.
Decide who will be A and who will be B.

A	[B]さんの かぞくは 何人 ですか。

B	四人 五人 六人	です。父と母と	おとうと あにが二人とあね あねといもうと あにとおとうと	が います。

A	そう ですか。ペット を かって いますか。

B	ええ、	いぬ ねこ	を	一ぴき 二ひき 三びき	かって います。

かぞくの しゃしん を みせましょうか。

A	ええ、みせて ください。この 人 は だれ?

B	あね あに いもうと おとうと	です。	しょうがく 二ねんせい ちゅうがく 一ねんせい こうこう 三ねんせい	です。

A	そう ですか。	せが たかい めが おおきい きれい ハンサム	ですね。	マスクを して いますね。 スキー を して いますね。 じょうば を して いますね。 え を かいて いますね。

B	ええ、	スポーツ がすき です。 どうぶつ がすき です。 え が じょうず です。 せんしゅう かぜ を ひいて いました。

A	へえ... この 人 は お父さん ですね。

B	はい、父 は いま	イギリス アメリカ ヨーロッパ 日本	に います。		A	あ、そう ですか。

いってみましょう

— ごかぞく は 何人 ですか。

（一）

かぞく は 四人 です。父 と 母 と
あね が います。あね の なまえ
は ひろこです。

（二）

ぼく の かぞく は 三人 です。父 と 母 と
ぼく です。ぼく は 二さい です。

（三）

かぞく は 四人 です。父 と 母 と
いもうと が います。いもうと の
りえこ は 六さい です。いぬ を
一ぴき かって います。

（四）

かぞく は 五人 です。父 と
おじいちゃん と おばあちゃん が
います。そして ひいおばあちゃん
も います。ひいおばあちゃん は
八十二さい です。

| ひいおばあちゃん | great grandmother |

These people have told you about their families. Ask your friend about his or her family.
You might ask questions such as:

・ごかぞく は 何人 ですか。
・おにいさん は 何さいですか。
・いもうとさん は 何ねんせい ですか。
・ペット を かって いますか。

Your class has been commissioned by a leading Japanese pet food manufacturer to find out which is the most popular pet food. In groups of 5 or 6, find out:

· who has pets and what they are
· which brand of food each pet eats

When you have collected this information, you should enter your findings on a table like the one below. The manufacturer can then analyse your results.

なまえ	ペット	ペット フード
ピーター	いぬ	Frend
サリー	ねこ	Purr
マーク	いぬ	Frend と Chew
	ねこ / 二ひき	Purr

日本語 ノート

■ Where are they?

The verb います means *be (in a place)*. When you use います to tell where people or animals are, you must put に after the place.

e.g. ケンくん は こうてい に います。
Ken is in the school ground.

いません is the negative form of います. You can use it to say that someone is not there.

e.g. たろうくん は へや に いますか。
Is Taroo in his room?
いいえ、いません。
No, he's not.

If you want to give more detailed information about where people (or animals) are, you can use expressions like:

まりこさんは みせのまえ に います。
Mariko is in front of the shop.
へび は いすのした に います。
The snake is under the chair.

You can also use です instead of (に) います to find out where people or animals are.

e.g. アマンダさん は どこ ですか。
Where's Amanda?
としょかん です。
She's in the library.

います cannot be used to tell where things are.

■ Talking about your family

います is also used when you are talking about your family and giving details. In this case います means *have*. You must put が after the person.

e.g. いもうと が います。
I have a little sister.

If you have more than one sister, you must include the number using the counting system for people, 一人 (ひとり), 二人 (ふたり), 三人 (さんにん), 四人 (よにん) etc. To explain that you have two younger sisters, you would say いもうと が 二人 います.

The counter for people comes before the verb.

おとうと が 一人 います。

いぬ を かって います。
I have a dog.
びょういん は こんで います。
The hospital is crowded.

はらじゅく は こんで いますね。

三　Talking about your pets

When you want to say how many pets you have, you must use the -ひき, -びき, -ぴき counter for animals. This counter comes before the verb.

e.g. いぬ を 三びき かって います。
　　 I have three dogs.

(If you do not have any pets, you can simply say ペット を かって いません。)

四　More about て います

In Unit 2, you learnt that a verb in て form followed by います tells us what someone is doing now. However, sometimes て います is used for an action or a state over a longer period. Look at these て います forms:

　　おなか が すいて います。
　　I am hungry.
　　かぜ を ひいて います。
　　I've got a cold.
　　よこはま に すんで います。
　　I live in Yokohama.

Remember that when you say this て います form, you need not pronounce い.

五　Saying what you don't do

The -ません form of the verb tells what you don't do.

e.g. あした がっこう に いきません。
　　 I'm not going to school tomorrow.

六　ごかぞく

When you ask someone who is older, or unknown to you, about their family, it is more polite to say ごかぞく.

e.g. やまださん、ごかぞく は 何人 ですか。
　　 How many people in your family, Mr Yamada?

七　More about と

と is a useful word that means both *and* and *with*. Compare these two sentences:

　　父 と 母 とあね が います。
　　(In my family,) there's my dad, mum and my older sister.
　　ともだち と さんぽ に いきました。
　　I went for a walk with my friends.

せいかつ

Hi everyone,

Big news! I've just found out that I'm related to a superstar. Well, almost. It's Yoko Tanaka. You know, Tanaka, as in Mr and Mrs Tanaka, the people I'm staying with. Yoko is their cousin or their niece or something. Well, I'm pretty sure she is, anyway.

I suppose you haven't heard of her. You know how in my last letter I told you I went to see Madonna in concert, well, what I didn't tell you is that Japan has its own pop industry and people here probably buy more Japanese records than ones from America, England or Australia. I've included a cutting from a Japanese pop magazine to give you an idea of how everyone is into it over here and to prove what I'm saying about Yoko Tanaka is all true. Her name is written in ローマじ on the poster too. The かんじ for Tanaka Yoko is 田中陽子.

I actually met Yoko a couple of times and she just seemed like any other Japanese teenager to me. I didn't even know she was training to be a star. You see, what happens here is that you get selected at an audition by one of the big recording companies and they work really hard to make you into a star. They put you through this really intensive instruction program, including voice and dance lessons, aerobics, public relations, fashion — everything you need to know about how to be an アイドル かしゅ. If you don't make it through the program you just go back to school and go on with your work. If they decide to package you as a star, then you get a chance to really make it big. That's what has happened to Yoko. One day nobody has heard of her, the next day she is everywhere!

She has a regular spot on Japan Sunday Hit Paradise and she is going to be in this new soapie called Top Stewardess. There's even going to be a special animated program about Yoko on Tuesdays at six o'clock. You can buy Yoko posters and even Yoko telephone cards. And like all the new アイドル かしゅ — there are about 75 of them introduced each year — she has made an 'image video'. We had a look at Yoko's video last night. It made her out to be super-cute, innocent, lovable girl-next-door, with typical teenage problems. That's so we can all identify with her, I suppose. And with her debut single you get a personal profile that includes her name, age, birthplace, hobbies, and even her bloodgroup! The bloodgroup is supposed to tell you a lot about a person's character or personality.

If everything goes well for Yoko, if her career really takes off, she will become like a goddess, a role model for every teenage girl. They will hang on every word she says and imitate the way she dresses. But if people just don't buy the 'package', then Yoko will just go back to school and get on with ordinary life. A lot of these overnight sensations seem to come and go all the time. She should make sure she continues her studies anyway, because she'll be finished by the time she's about 19 or 20. All the アイドル かしゅ are. When they reach that age, they just farewell all the millions of adoring fans and get married and have children.

Actually, she will have quite a lot of competition. The かわいい idol singers aren't quite as popular as they used to be. Their place is being taken by singing groups and by bands. I've included a couple of fan cards to give you the idea. You can buy these photos everywhere.

This is Wink. Wink is really popular here at the moment. When they sing they do all these complicated hand movements in time together and of course all the fans imitate them. Everyone does it. It's funny to see a businessman in a suit in his car stopped at a traffic-light start to do these movements when a Wink song comes on the radio.

This card is of ひで, a member of X. I saw one of their concerts at the とうきょう ドーム on TV. One thing I can say about their music is it was LOUD! You couldn't really hear what they were singing but everyone in the audience was getting up and dancing and clapping. That's what is called the スピード feeling and that's what

the new bands try to give their audiences. A lot of the bands sing quite a lot of English words but the thing is, they don't mean anything. They really don't. Sometimes people at school ask me what the words mean, and when I can't make any sense of them they think it's because I don't know Japanese well enough to translate properly, and they go away really disappointed. I mean, what would you make of this? 'Positive dance, friend feel'. Now when anyone asks me I just make something up like 'I really love you baby' and everyone is happy.

Even though they are getting away a little bit from the かわいい image for their stars, the bands just can't bring themselves to be anti-fashionable. There is a new all-female band called Princess Princess and they have a really great sound, I think. But everyone I hear talking about them discusses what they wear and how they want to get way-out dresses just like them. I sometimes think they are just as much fashion models as singers.

Anyway, we're all hoping that Yoko Tanaka can stay on top for a few years. If she doesn't, it won't be the fault of her managers at the record company. They have proclaimed every 8th day of the month 'Yoko Day'. I'll be doing my bit to help her. I'll be in my Yoko Tanaka T・シャツ with my Yoko Tanaka badge, have my B2-size poster on my wall and buy all the products that she advertises in the TV commercials.

Anyway, must dash － Top Stewardess is coming on TV. If I miss it, I won't know what everyone is talking about at school tomorrow.

Lots of love,
Simone シモーン

P.S. Don't forget, 'Positive dance, friend feel'.

単語

1	いっぴき	一ぴき
2	にひき	二ひき
3	さんびき	三びき
4	よんひき	四ひき
5	ごひき	五ひき
6	ろっぴき	六ぴき
7	ななひき	七ひき
8	はっぴき	八ぴき
9	きゅうひき	九ひき
10	じゅっぴき	十ぴき

1	ひとり	一人
2	ふたり	二人
3	さんにん	三人
4	よにん	四人
5	ごにん	五人
6	ろくにん	六人
7	しちにん	七人
8	はちにん	八人
9	きゅうにん	九人
10	じゅうにん	十人

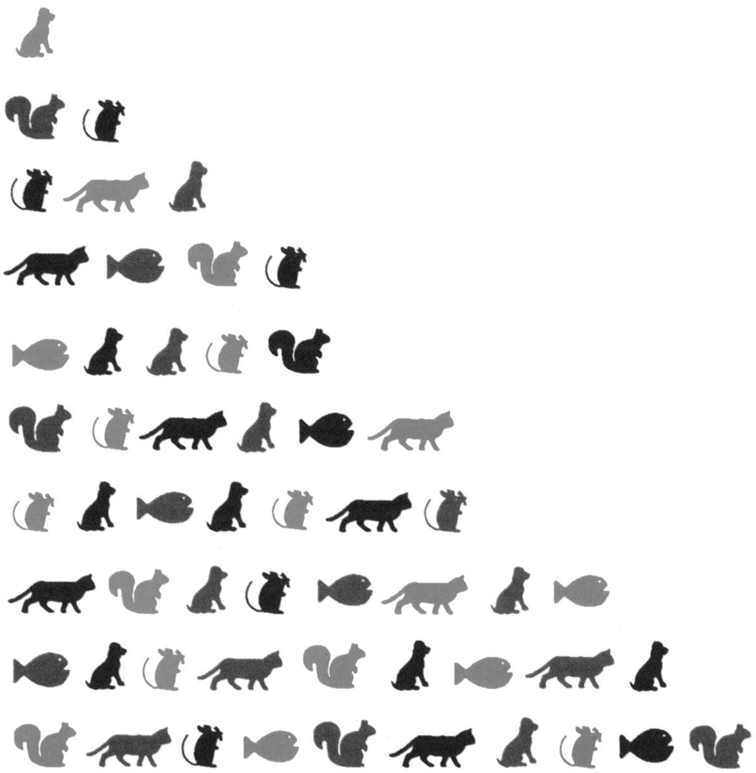

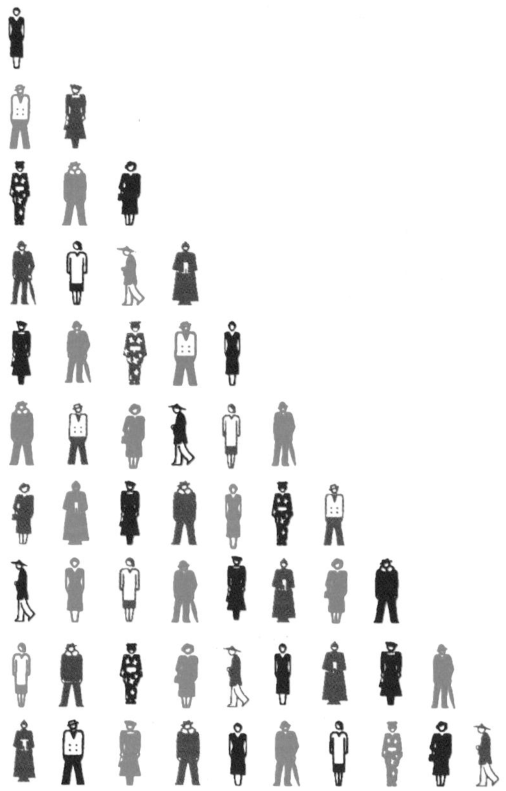

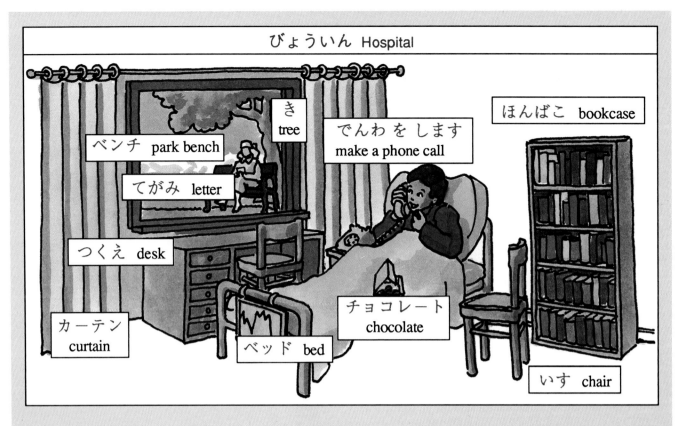

びょういん Hospital

- き tree
- ベンチ park bench
- でんわ を します make a phone call
- ほんばこ bookcase
- てがみ letter
- つくえ desk
- チョコレート chocolate
- カーテン curtain
- ベッド bed
- いす chair

どうぶつ Animals		
かめ	__	tortoise
さかな	__	fish
ぶた	__	pig

Locations		
うえ	__	on, above, up
うしろ	__	behind
した	__	under, below, down
まえ	__	in front of
きょうしつ	__	classroom

Expressions		
おなか が すいて いますか。	__	are you hungry?
こら!	__	you're in big trouble!
こんで います	__	it's crowded
たくさん	__	lots, many
なまけもの	__	lazy, lazy thing
はずかしかった	__	how embarrassing
ふとりすぎ	__	he's too fat
わたし じゃない	__	not me

おめでとう!

You are now able to use your 日本語 to:

- ask and tell where people and animals are
- give information about your family
- ask someone about their family and pets
- talk about your pets
- count people and animals
- talk about things that you don't do much

第五課・ドーナツ は ぜんぜん 食べません。

もくようびの 四じ

マイクくん、ドーナツ は いかが ですか。

ぼく… ドーナツ は ぜんぜん 食べません。

ぜんぜん?

ぜんぜん。

あら、トライアスロン たいかい? その トライアスロン に 行きますか。

はい、いま まいにち トレーニング を して います。

トレーニング を ? へえ… どんな トレーニング?

まいにち 五じ二十ぷん に おきて、トレーナー を きます。

五じ二十ぷん? はやい ですね。

ええ。そして トレーニング シューズ を はいて、五じ三十五ふん に ランニング に 行きます。 十キロメートル はしります。

へええ? 十キロ? すごい!

シャワー を あびて、あさごはん を 食べます。 コーンフレーク を 食べて、オレンジ ジュース を のみます。

ときどき 十二キロ はしります。それから、プール で 三びゃく メートル およいで、うち に かえります。

わたしも ときどき あさ およぎます。マイクくん、あさごはん は?

それから、八じ 五ふん に じてんしゃ で がっこう に 行きます。

きんようびの はじはん

ねえ、みんな。マイクくんは すごい
ですよ。まいあさ五じに おきて、
二十キロ はしります。それから
五ひゃく メートルおよぎます。

ほんとうかなあ??

ほんとう ですよ。
マイクくんは にちようびの
トライアスロン たいかい に
行きます。
みんな、行きませんか。

たいかいですか。

いい ですね。行きましょう。

にちようびの はじはん

わあー!すごい!人 が たくさん いますね。

マイクくんは ?

ホット ドッグ!ホット ドッグ は
いかが? アイスクリーム、ドーナツ、
ミート パイ は いかがですか。

あっ、マイクくん?

マイクくんは すごい ですね。
チャンピオン ですね。

アマンダさん、
ドーナツ は
いかが ですか。

ドーナツ?食べませんよ!!

いいましょう ー

Using the example as a guide, talk about what time おさむくん got up during last week.

例:

> A きんようび に 何じ に おきましたか。
> B 六じ 四十五ふん に おきました。

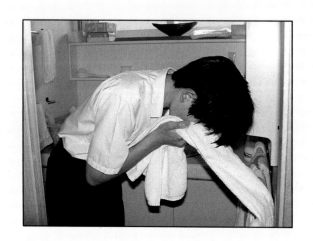

いいましょう 二

 10 キロ　　 300 メートル　　

 100 メートル　　 2 キロ　　

　　　　 100 メートル　　 1 キロ

 50 メートル　　 25 メートル　　

　　　　 3 キロ　　 200 メートル

Using the example as a guide, talk about each character's training program.

例:

A マイクくん、どんな トレーニング を しますか。
B 10キロ はしって、三びゃく メートル およぎます。
　それ から エアロビクス を します。

いいましょう 三

ようふく

ポロシャツ

トレーナー

トレパン

スニーカー

パーカ

ジャケット

ジーンズ

スカーフ

セーター

スカート

パジャマ

第五課 ● 六十六

ジージャン

ベルト

ショート
パンツ

ハイソックス

ショートブーツ

バスケット
シューズ

スリッパ

トレーニング
シューズ

シャツ

Tシャツ

タンクトップ

パンツ

スカート

ワンピース

カーディガン

Using the example as a guide, discuss the clothes in the catalogue.

例:

A すてき な ポロシャツ ですね。 B ええ、 [A] さん は ときどき ポロシャツ を きますか。 A ええ、よく きます。 　or A いいえ、ぜんぜん きません。 　　　あまり
A すてき な ジーンズ ですね。 B ええ、 [A] さん は ときどき ジーンズ を はきますか。 A ええ、よく はきます。 　or A いいえ、ぜんぜん はきません。 　　　あまり

きせつ

はなこさん and ゆうこさん are giving a talk about the seasons in Japan.

はる spring	
三月	March
四月	April
五月	May

あき autumn	
九月	September
十月	October
十一月	November

ふゆ winter	
十二月	December
一月	January
二月	February

なつ summer	
六月	June
(つゆ rainy season)	
七月	July
八月	August

あき
あき は すずしい です。九月 に
ときどき たいふう が きます。
十一月 に やま で
こうよう を 見ます。
とても きれい です。

ふゆ
ふゆ は さむい です。
たまに とうきょう で
ゆき が ふります。
ほっかいどう では ゆき
が たくさん ふります。
よく やま に 行って、
スキー を します。

なつ
日本 の なつ は あつい です。
六月 は つゆ です。まいにち
あめ が ふります。
いやです よ。七月 と
八月 は なつ やすみ
です。よく うみ で
すいえい を します。
そして やま に
ハイキング に 行きます。

はる
はる は あたたかい
です。四月 に
はなみ を
します。
きのした に
すわって、ピクニック を します。
はなみ の おべんとう は おいしい
です。たのしい です よ。

すずしい ___ cool		さむい ___ cold	
たいふう ___ typhoon		ゆき が ふります ___ it snows	
こうよう ___ autumn colours		あたたかい ___ warm	
つゆ ___ rainy season		はなみ ___ flower viewing	
あめ が ふります ___ it rains		おべんとう ___ a boxed lunch	

ともだちと

Make up a conversation with a partner. Decide who will be A and who will be B.

こうてい で　A| [B]さん、| どうしたん ですか。
|| [B]くん、|

B| のど | が いたいん です。| いま かぜを ひいて います。
| あし || きのう から てを しました。
| おなか || きのう チョコレートを たくさん たべました。

A| そうですか。じゃ | うちに かえりますか。
|| びょういんに 行きますか。

B| いいえ、| サッカー | の トレーニングに 行きます。
	バスケット
	けんどう
	すいえい

らいしゅう クラブ の キャンプに 行きます。

A| いいですね。

B| よくない ですよ。まいにち あさの 五じ十ぷんに おきて | トレーニングを します。
||| 十キロ はしります。
||| プールで およぎます。

A| へええ?

B| [A]さん、| すてきな | テニス シューズ | を はいて いますね。
| [A]くん、| いい | バスケット シューズ | を きて いますね。
||| パーカ |
||| スポーツ シャツ |

[A]さん | は どんな スポーツを しますか。
[A]くん

A| スポーツは | すきじゃない です。| でも、この | テニス シューズ | は
	ぜんぜん しません。		バスケット シューズ
	あまり しません。		パーカ
				スポーツ シャツ

かっこいい ですね。

せいかつ

がくねん(学年)　School year

四月
日 月 火 水 木 金 土
1 2 3 4 5 6
7 8 9 10 11 12 13
14 15 16 17 18 19 20
21 22 23 24 25 26 27
28 29 30

四月 に にゅうがく
しき(入学式) が
あります。
一ねんせい は
あたらしい
せいふく を きて、
がっこう に きます。

にゅうがく しき　new student entrance ceremony
あります　there is

五月
日 月 火 水 木 金 土
1 2 3 4
5 6 7 8 9 10 11
12 13 14 15 16 17 18
19 20 21 22 23 24 25
26 27 28 29 30 31

五月 に しけん が
あります。せいと
は がんばって、
べんきょう します。

しけん　exams
しゅうがく
りょこう　school trip

三ねんせい は
しゅうがく
りょこう
(修学旅行) に
行きます。

六月
日 月 火 水 木 金 土
30 　 　 　 　 　 1
2 3 4 5 6 7 8
9 10 11 12 13 14 15
16 17 18 19 20 21 22
23 24 25 26 27 28 29

六月 は つゆ です。まいにち
あめ が ふります。

七月
日 月 火 水 木 金 土
1 2 3 4 5 6
7 8 9 10 11 12 13
14 15 16 17 18 19 20
21 22 23 24 25 26 27
28 29 30 31

インターハイ の きせつ です。

		八月				
日	月	火	水	木	金	土
					1	2	3
4	5	6	7	8	9	10
11	12	13	14	15	16	17
18	19	20	21	22	23	24
25	26	27	28	29	30	31

なつやすみ です。
クラブの れんしゅう と
キャンプ を します。

れんしゅう practice
はじまります begin

		九月				
日	月	火	水	木	金	土
1	2	3	4	5	6	7
8	9	10	11	12	13	14
15	16	17	18	19	20	21
22	23	24	25	26	27	28
29	30					

がっこう は はじまります。

		十月				
日	月	火	水	木	金	土
		1	2	3	4	5
6	7	8	9	10	11	12
13	14	15	16	17	18	19
20	21	22	23	24	25	26
27	28	29	30	31		

しけん が あります。 そして スポーツ ディ
も あります。 がんばれ!

		十一月				
日	月	火	水	木	金	土
					1	2	3
4	5	6	7	8	9	10
11	12	13	14	15	16	17
18	19	20	21	22	23	24
25	26	27	28	29	30	

ぶんかさい cultural festival

ぶんかさい(文化祭)か コンサート が あります。
たのしい ですよ。

		十二月				
日	月	火	水	木	金	土
30	31					1
2	3	4	5	6	7	8
9	10	11	12	13	14	15
16	17	18	19	20	21	22
23	24	25	26	27	28	29

ふゆ やすみ に
クリスマス と
おしょうがつ が
あります。
ときどき スキー に
行きます。

		一月				
日	月	火	水	木	金	土
		1	2	3	4	5
6	7	8	9	10	11	12
13	14	15	16	17	18	19
20	21	22	23	24	25	26
27	28	29	30	31		

三ねんせい の
しけん が
あります。

おしょうがつ New Year

		二月				
日	月	火	水	木	金	土
					1	2
3	4	5	6	7	8	9
10	11	12	13	14	15	16
17	18	19	20	21	22	23
24	25	26	27	28		

三月 に そつぎょうしき
(卒業式) が あります。
はるやすみ は はじまります。

そつぎょうしき graduation ceremony

がんばれ

Active listening

The first thing that strikes you when you hear two Japanese people conversing is that the listener seems to have nearly as much to say as the speaker. A Japanese listener always takes an active part in a conversation, chiming in with ああ、そう and そう です か. These are just two of the 'response expressions' that are used in Japanese to show interest in what is being said and to encourage the speaker to go on. Do we have anything like this in English?

This practice is even more noticeable during telephone conversations in Japanese. Since the listener can't be seen, he or she works overtime on the 'response expressions' and may show agreement by saying そう そう そう! If the speaker feels a lack of this sort of listener feedback, he or she will check that the other person is still on the line with an urgent cry of もし もし. Does anything like this happen during English telephone conversations?

Take every opportunity to use these response expressions, especially during いって みま しょう activities. They offer you a fun way of sounding genuinely Japanese. But don't forget to pay attention to intonation, i.e. the tone of voice that you use. For example, そう です か can mean that you are really interested or that you doubt the truth of what is being said. It all depends on how you say it. Here are some other, similar expressions that you know.

そう です ね	to show that you agree, or that at least you're thinking about it
へえ?	to show that you are surprised or impressed
ほんとう?	to show that you doubt the truth of what is being said or that you are surprised

So, don't forget: even when your main job is to listen, you still have to hold up your end of a Japanese conversation.

いってみましょう

へえ?

Make up ten sentences describing things that you do. These could include your morning routine, or your weekend activities. Try to include the times when you do these things. Don't feel tied down by the truth － let your imagination run free! Your friend will respond to your statements using some response expressions. He or she might use those below.

いい です ね。_____	That sounds good!
はやい です ね。_____	That's early!
わたしも、ぼくも。_____	Me too.
うそ です。_____	That's a lie! I don't believe you!
ほんとう? _____	Really?
そう です か。_____	Yeah?

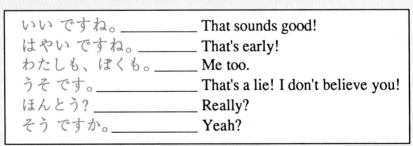

まいあさ 五じ に
おきますよ。

へえ? ほんとう?

Have your partner tell you his or her statements and respond appropriately.

日本語 ノート

一 Telling the time

You already know how to tell the time on the hour and half-hour. To tell the time in intervals of 5 minutes, you use 五ふん (ごふん), which means five minutes.
Look at these examples.

いま 六じ 五ふん ですね。
It's now 6.05.
七じ 十五ふん に あいましょう。
Let's meet at 7.15.

十ぷん (じゅっぷん) means ten minutes and you can use this to tell the time in 10-minute intervals.

いま 九じ 十ぷん ですね。
It's now 9.10.
十じ 四十ぷん に 行きましょう。
Let's go at 10.40.

When you want to meet your friend at 7.50, you can say,

七じ 五十ぷん に あいましょう。
Let's meet at 7.50.
or
八じ 十ぷん まえ に あいましょう。
Let's meet at 10 to 8.

まえ means *in front of* or *before*. If you are doing something at a particular time, don't forget to use に after the time.

二 Getting dressed

There are several verbs that are used in 日本語 to talk about what you are wearing. The two most common ones are きます and はきます. When you wear items that you put your arms through, きます is used.

e.g. おもしろい T・シャツ を きて いますね。
You're wearing an interesting T-shirt.

Anything that you wear on the lower part of your body uses はきます.

e.g. あたらしい くつ を はいて います。
I'm wearing new shoes.

きます is used for clothing like a suit, a uniform or pyjamas. します can be used for a tie, belt or jewellery.

e.g. ときどき イヤリング を します。
I sometimes wear earrings.

三 More about the て form

To talk about a series of actions, you can use the て form of the verb. In this case, the て form has the meaning of the verb plus *and*.

e.g. きのう まち へ 行って、おもしろい えいが を 見ました。
Yesterday I went to town and saw a great film.
まいあさ シャワー を あびて、せいふく を きて、がっこう に 行きます。
Every morning I have a shower, put on my uniform and go to school.

The word それから, which means *after that* and そして, which means *and then*, are also useful for talking about the order of events.

四 あまり、ぜんぜん

When you want to say that you don't do something very often or you never do it, you use あまり and ぜんぜん with the verb in the negative -ません form.

e.g. よく テニス を しますか。
Do you play tennis often?
いいえ、あまり しません。
No, not very often.
いいえ、ぜんぜん しません。
No, never.

あまり is another way of saying あんまり. When you answer a question like おすし は すき ですか with いいえ、あんまり... you are shortening the statement いいえ、あんまり すき じゃない です。

単語

Time じかん

五十五ふん 55
五ふんまえ 5 to

五ふん
5 past

五十ぷん 50
十ぷん まえ 10 to

十ぷん
10 past

四十五ふん 45
十五ふん まえ
quarter to

十五ふん
quarter past

四十ぷん 40
二十ぷん まえ
20 to

二十ぷん
20 past

三十五ふん 35
二十五ふん まえ 25 to

二十五ふん
25 past

三十ぷん 30
はん half past

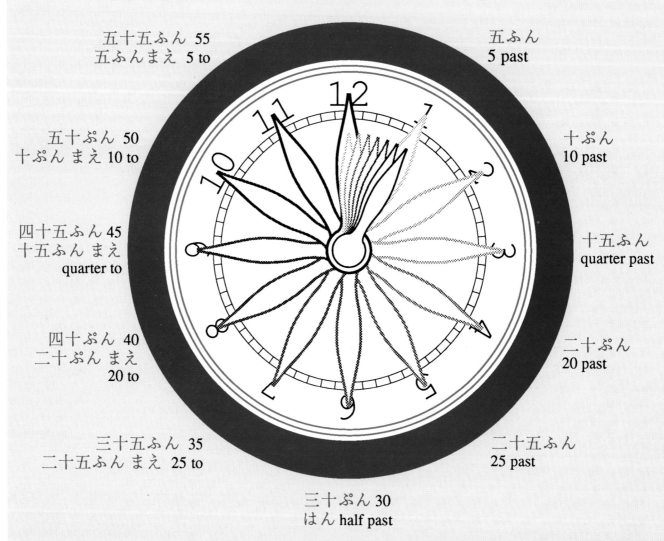

いま 何じ ですか。

New words

あまり —	not often
いつも —	always
ぜんぜん —	never
たまに —	occasionally
ときどき —	sometimes
まい... —	every...
まいにち —	every day
よく —	often

あさ —	morning
あさごはん —	breakfast
せいふく —	school uniform
そして —	and then
どんな —	what kind of?

カタカナの 単語

アイスクリーム —	ice-cream
オレンジ ジュース —	orange juice
キロ(メートル) —	kilo(metre)
コーンフレーク —	cornflakes
トライアスロン —	triathlon
トレーニング —	training
ドーナツ —	doughnut
ホット ドッグ —	hot dog
ミートパイ —	meat pie

Verbs

WEAK

(シャワー を)	
あびます —	take (a shower)
おきます —	wake up, get up
きます —	put on, wear (top part of body)

STRONG

はしります —	run
およぎます —	swim
はきます —	put on, wear (lower part of body)

Numbers 100－1,000

百	— 100	— ひゃく
二百	— 200	— にひゃく
三百	— 300	— さんびゃく
四百	— 400	— よんひゃく
五百	— 500	— ごひゃく
六百	— 600	— ろっぴゃく
七百	— 700	— ななひゃく
八百	— 800	— はっぴゃく
九百	— 900	— きゅうひゃく
	1000	— せん

いかが ですか。
How about this?

おめでとう！

You are now able to use your 日本語 to:

· talk about what you wear and don't wear
· talk about your morning routine
· tell someone what time it is (in 5- and 10-minute intervals)
· count to 1000
· talk about how often you do things

第六課・ベビー シッター は らくだなあ！

テリーくん は スケート ボード が じょうず ですね。

いいえ、そう でも ない ですよ。

あのう、テリーくん、こんばん ひま ですか。

うん。どうして?

ええと、こんばん でかけます。ベビー シッター を して くれませんか。

えっ?ぼく?ベビー シッター?

テリーくん、おねがい！おねがい！おねがい！

オッケー

KOTSU KOTSU

こどもたち は ばんごはん を もう 食べました。いつも 七じはん に おふろ に はいります。そして 八じはん に ねます。

リーちゃん、エミちゃん、ボールあそびをしてはだめですよ。テレビのへやで食べてはだめですよ。

テリーくんのごはんはれいぞうこのなかにあります。食べてね。

テレビを見てもいいですか。

ええ、もちろんいいですよ。

あのファミコンをつかってもいいですか。

ええ、どうぞ。

わたしたちは　十一じはんにかえります。じゃ、おねがいします。

テリーくん、テレビのへやで食べてはだめですよ。

もう　七じ二十ぷんですよ。おふろにはいって。

オッケー!

シャンプーをつかってもいい?

いいよ。

ベビーシッターはらくだなあ。

えっ、?

パジャマをきて。

パジャマはドライヤのなかにあります。とって。

はい、パジャマ。きて ください。

その パジャマ じゃ ない です。あかい パジャマ は すき じゃ ない です。

きいろい パジャマ は きらい です。

あおい パジャマ も きらい です。

うるさい!

お父さんの パジャマ...

ビデオ を 見て も いい?

だめ。

ボール あそび も だめ!

おなか が すいて ます。ホット ケーキ を つくって も いい?

だめ! ばんごはん を もう 食べましたね。

いいえ、まだ です。

うそ!

いいましょう 一

Using the example as a guide, ask permission to do or make use of various things.

例：

A ファミコン を つかっても いい ですか。
B ええ、いい です。 （どうぞ）
  or
  いいえ、だめ です。

Using the example as a guide, give permission to do or make use of various things.

例：

ファミコン を つかっても いい です。

Using the example as a guide, talk about how often you do or make use of various things.

例：

A よく ファミコン を つかい ますか。
B ええ、よく つかい ます。 （だい すき です）
  or
  いいえ、ぜんぜん つかい ません。 （きらい です）

These verbs might be of use	
つかいます	のみます
つくります	はきます
見ます	食べます

いいましょう 二

Using the example as a guide, tell these children that they are not allowed to do these things.

例:

> ピアノ を ひいて は だめ です。

Using the example as a guide, comment on the behaviour of these children.

例:

> A あのこ は ピアノ を ひいて います。
> B ひどい です ね。ピアノ を ひいて は だめ です。

This is a sign from an art classroom.
What do you think is だめ in this room?

⊠⊠

いいましょう 三

Using the example as a guide, talk about the colour of these clothes.

例:

| A　このジャケット は何いろ ですか。 |
| B　あかい です。 |

Using the example as a guide, talk about whether you like these clothes.

例:

A あかい ジャケット は すき ですか。
B ええ、すき です。
　　or
　　いいえ、すき じゃない です。
　　or
　　いいえ、きらい です。

Using the example as a guide, talk about the colour of the advertised items.

例:

> A　この いろ は すき ですか。
> B　ブラック ですか。
> 　　はい、すき です。
> 　　or
> 　　いいえ、すき じゃない です。

東京 ディズニーランド の アンケート

This アンケート was compiled from the responses of students visiting 東京 ディズニーランド.

Q ディズニーランド へ 何かい 行きましたか。

A
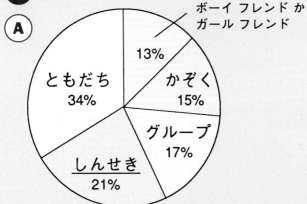

- >10 17%
- 7-9 15%
- 4-6 42%
- 1-3 26%

Q だれ と 行きましたか。

A

ボーイ フレンド か ガール フレンド 13%
- かぞく 15%
- グループ 17%
- しんせき 21%
- ともだち 34%

Q すき な アトラクション は 何 ですか。

A
1 スペース・マウンテン
2 ビッグサンダー・マウンテン

Q スナック は 何 を 食べましたか。

A
1 ポップコーン
2 アイスクリーム
3 クレープ

Q パレード を 見ましたか。

A
はい　　95%
いいえ　5%

Q おみやげ は 何 を かいましたか。

A
1 ぬいぐるみ
2 キーホルダー
3 おかし

Q いくら つかいましたか。

A
1 10,000ー15,000円　　49%
2 5,000ー10,000円　　40%
3 >15,000円　　　　　 9%

パス ポート が 4,000円,
のこりの 5,000円ー10,000 円が
食事代 と おみやげ代 に なります。

アンケート	___ survey
何かい	___ how many times?
しんせき	___ relatives
ぬいぐるみ	___ stuffed toys
いくら	___ how much?
円 (えん)	___ yen

ともだちと

Make up a conversation with a partner. Decide who will be A and who will be B.

A | お母さん、ただいま。

B | あ、 [B]さん、
[B]くん、 | おかえりなさい。 | やきゅうの トレーニング
えい語の テスト | は どうでしたか。

A | よかった
むずかしかった
すごかった | ですよ。お母さん、おなか が すいてます。

いま | ケーキ
サンドイッチ
ハンバーガー | を | 食べて も いい ですか。
つくって も いい ですか。

B | いいえ、だめ ですよ。 | りんご
オレンジ | を 食べて、 | シャワー を あびて ください。
おふろ に はいって ください。

こんばん | おばあさんの うちに 行きます。
レストラン で ばんごはんを 食べます。
お父さんと でかけます。

A | ああ、そう ですか。じゃ | ぼく
わたし | の あたらしい | ジーンズ
T・シャツ
テニス シューズ

を | きて も いい ですか。
はいて も いい ですか。

B | いいえ、だめ です。その | あかい
ピンクの
くろい | パンツ
シャツ
くつ | を | きて ください。
はいて ください。

A | お母さん...あれ は | すき じゃない
きらい | ですよ。

せいかつ

Hi everyone,

I told you it would happen. You know all that fuss they made about Yoko Tanaka's debut, well, she has almost disappeared from the scene. I guess they'll now have someone else starring on Top Stewardess and making a video and writing a book and selling heaps of records.

But that's not why I'm writing. Mr Tanaka has just got his mid-year bonus and he is letting us each choose a present. He's really nice, because he has included me as well. They really treat me like one of the family now.

I'm not exactly sure what the bonus is for, but Mr Tanaka explained that nearly all Japanese workers get a big part of their annual pay in one go. Actually, it happens twice a year, once at the start of summer and once just before Christmas. Everyone really looks forward to these bonus times and all the shops put out brochures full of ideas on how to spend all that money! I cut out a few bits from these brochures so you will know what I'm talking about in the rest of the letter.

Let's start with the youngest. Haruko has asked for a ROBO portable sing-along system. It's called a パーティカラオケ. The one she wants lets you be a からおけ singer and that's just what Haruko wants to be. She can't wait until she's old enough to go into a karaoke bar and show off her talent.

She just sings all the time now. It's all because cousin Yoko told her she was かわいい and that she had a nice voice. Anyway, in these bars the customers get up and sing along with recorded music. The good thing about ROBO is that you can press a button to get wild applause and people screaming 'Encore!' I wouldn't mind a go myself.

Toshio wants to get a ビデオウォークマン. He says it's just essential because there is nothing to look at when you are walking around or travelling in the train. He can just see himself riding along on his bike, watching one of his favourite videos. Could be interesting! He wants the one you can plug into the car stereo system.

ビデオウォークマン

I'm next. What I really want is a ラップトップ ワープロ. It would be just great to be able to carry it around anywhere and do assignments and that.

パーティカラオケ

パーティー
スイッチ
「アンコール」
「ファンファーレ」

スピード
コントロール

エコー

ROBO

ラップトップワープロ

I could even write these letters on the train on the way to school. But I don't think it would be fair to ask for that, so I'm going to go for a コピー ペン. *They're just amazing. You just run them over some lines in a book, say, and then it will copy them into your notebook. It should be great for taking study notes, and if I ever go into the spy business.*

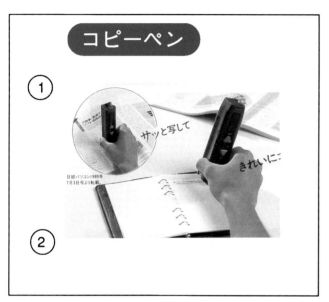

Mrs Tanaka is getting the most expensive thing. That's fair. It's a カラービデオプリンター. *It works like this. Say you're watching a video and you see something you really like. Well, you freeze that frame, press a button and out comes a colour print of it. Amazing! Mrs Tanaka wants it so she can get prints from family videos, like Haruko's birthday party last week. I suppose they could use the fantastic camera they have, but it's not my business, really.*

Poor Mr Tanaka is getting himself the most boring thing. It's called a パームトップ コンピューター *and as far as I can work out he can use it for business planning and records and communication and stuff like that. Anyway, I suppose he will have a go on the video printer when he feels like it.*

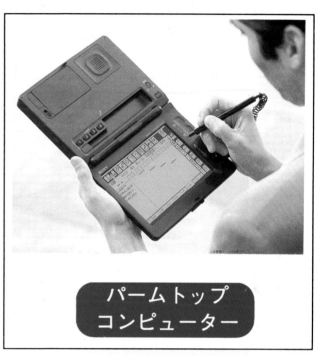

Well, I hope I haven't bored you with all this. I just thought you'd like to see what's around over here. Sometimes I wonder about it all, but I suppose it all helps to make life better. I don't know. What do you think?

Anyway, must dash. I just heard Haruko scream and I think that means that Mr Tanaka is just arriving home. He just might have his arms full, so I might go and help him.

バイバイ
シモーン より

P.S. I'll post this tomorrow. Tonight I want to copy some of it into my diary. Guess what I'll be using to do it.

いってみましょう

1 でかけて も いい です か。

You'd really like to go out with some friends, perhaps to see a film or have a pizza. You'll have to ask a parent permission for this and, of course, they will ask the usual questions, such as 'Where to? Who with? How will you get there? What time will you get home?' etc. etc...

Have your partner play the role of a concerned parent. If you can answer by making your parent feel confident that you are well organized, he or she will let you go. This means that you will have to answer without too much hesitation!

2 でんわ を つかって も いい です か。

Your parents are going overseas for six months and they are letting you choose a friend to live with.

Using a survey form like the one below, ask three friends if you'll be allowed to do these things at their place. Your friends should respond honestly, basing their answers on what they are permitted to do.

	ペニー	ロバート	ジョー
📺			
☎			
🍔			
🎸			
📼			
🎫			

Now that you have the answers, decide who you would prefer to move in with.

単語

何 いろ What colour?

あおい	___	blue
あかい	___	red
きいろい	___	yellow
くろい	___	black
しろい	___	white
ピンク(の)	___	pink
みどり(の)	___	green

Expressions

うん	___	yeah
きらい です	___	I hate it
して くれませんか	___	will you do this for me?
どうして？	___	why?
ドライヤ の なか	___	in the clothes-dryer
はやく	___	quickly, hurry up!
ひどい	___	dreadful, terrible, what a cheek!
もちろん	___	of course
らくだなあ	___	this is really easy, what a breeze!

New words

いっしょに	___	together
おふろ	___	bath
こどもたち	___	children
シャンプー	___	shampoo
ばんごはん	___	evening meal
ベビー シッター	___	baby-sitter
れいぞうこ	___	fridge
わたしたち	___	we

Verbs

でかけます	___	go out
ねます	___	go to bed, go to sleep

あります	___	there is, be (in a place)
つくります	___	make
とります	___	take
はいります	___	enter, go in
つかいます	___	use

おふろ に はいって います。

シャワー を あびて います。

日本語 ノート

一 Asking permission

When you ask permission to do something, you add も いい です か to the て form of the verb.

e.g. パーティー に 行って も いい です か。

May I go to the party?

If you are allowed to go, then your parent may say

ええ、いい です。
Yes, that's OK.

If you are told, いいえ、だめ です, you are not allowed to go.

If you wish to tell someone that it is OK for them to do something, you can use this permission form without か.

e.g ジーンズ を はいて も いい です。
It's OK to wear jeans.

二 Saying something is forbidden

When you want to say quite strongly that something is not allowed, は だめ です is added to the て form of the verb.

e.g. はしって は だめ です!
No running!
この みせ で 食べて は だめ です。
You're not allowed to eat in this shop.

三 Love it or hate it?

In 日本語, as in English, there are many ways of saying how much you like or dislike something. Look at the list below:

だいすき	I really like it, I love it
すき	I like it
(あんまり) すき じゃない	I'm not that keen on it, I don't like it
きらい	I hate it
だい きらい	I can't stand it, I loathe it

People generally use (あんまり) すき じゃない when they don't like something, rather than the stronger words きらい and だいきらい.

四 何 いろ です か。

Just when you thought you knew many colours in 日本語, you pick up a magazine or brochure and notice words like レッド and ブルー being used instead of あかい and あおい.
Just as in English when we use words like 'champagne' or 'milkwood' to describe beige and off-white, it is very popular in Japanese advertising to use the English colour words.

Colours that don't end in い are nouns in 日本語 and so の is used.

e.g. みどり の セーター を かいました。
I bought a green jumper.

おめでとう!

You are now able to use your 日本語 to:

· ask if you may do something
· tell someone what they are allowed to do
· tell someone what they must not do
· talk about how much you like or dislike something
· describe something using a colour

第七課 ・ この いす の あし は ありますか。

あ、きょう は ガレージ セール です ね。

わあ、何、これ!? これ を うります か。ひどい ね。

うち に ふるい もの が たくさん あります。

ガレージ セール

わあー! すごい! りっぱな ゴルフ クラブ です ね。これ を うります か。

ええ、うち に たくさん あります。

それ は 何 です か。

でんき スタンド です。

ランプ シェード は どこ に あります か。

アマンダさん の あたま の うえ に あります。

何、それ？きたないね。ひどいね。

ふるい たんす ですね。それ をうりますか。

うえき はいくら ですか。

うえき はぜんぶ 一ドル です。

じゃ、それ を ください。

ありがとう ございます。

ああ...

この いす のあし は ありますか。

ええと...

このくまのて は ありますか。

ボール はどこ ですか。

このベッドの マットレス は?

ゴルフ バッグ は ありますか。

この たんす を 見て。
りっぱ ですね。

ええ、すばらしい
アンチック ですよ。

いらっしゃいませ。

あの たんす は いくら ですか。

五ドル です。

五ドル!? ほんとうかな。
しんじられない! やすいね。

ほんとうに
五ドル ですか。
しんじられない...

そう ですか。
たかい?
じゃ 四ドル。

四ドル? それは...

オッケー! しょうがない。
三ドル!

ほんとう? じゃ、どうぞ。

テリーくん! わたし
の たんす は どこ?

あの ふるい たんす ですか。
もう うりましたよ。はい、
どうぞ。三ドル です。

あああ...

Using the example as a guide, talk about the location of each shop.

例：

> A やおや は どこ に ありますか。
> B やおや ですか。やおや は にくや の となり に あります。
>   or
>   やおや は おかしや と にくや の あいだ に あります。

Using the example as a guide, talk about where things are.

例:

> A ポスト は どこ ですか。
> B パンや の まえ です。

Using the example as a guide, talk about your shopping.

例:

> A その バナナ を どこ で 買いましたか。
> B あの やおや で 買いました。

いいましょう 二

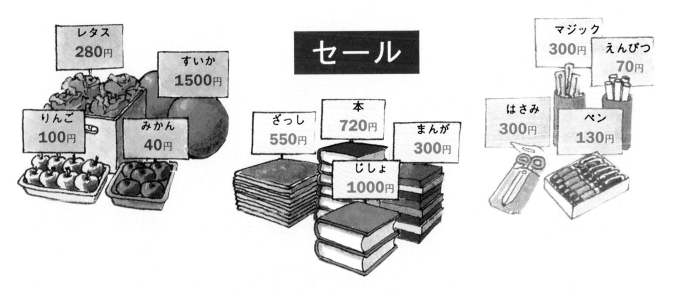

レタス 280円

すいか 1500円

りんご 100円

みかん 40円

セール

ざっし 550円

本 720円

まんが 300円

じしょ 1000円

マジック 300円

えんぴつ 70円

はさみ 300円

ペン 130円

Using the example as a guide, do a stock-take in each section.

例:

> A 本 は 何さつ ありますか。
> B 六さつ あります。
>
> A レタス は いくつ ありますか。
> B 四つ あります。
>
> A マジック は 何本 あります か。
> B 三本 あります。

Using the example as a guide, find out if the item is in stock and buy it.

例:

> A はさみ は ありますか。
> B はい、あります。
> A じゃ、それ を ください。

Using the example as a guide, find out the price of the item.

例:

> A はさみ は いくら ですか。
> B 300 円 です。

Using the example as a guide, buy the items.

例:

> A りんご を 五つ ください。
> B はい。
> 　 じゃ、ぜんぶで 500 円 です。

ともだちと

Make up a conversation with a partner. Decide who will be A and who will be B.

アイスクリーム の みせで

A | いらっしゃいませ。

B | チョコ チップ / パイナップル | の アイスクリーム は ありますか。

A | すみません、きょう | チョコ チップ / パイナップル | は ありません。

B | ああ、そう。じゃ、その | ピンク の / グリーン の / イエロー の | アイスクリーム は 何 ですか。

A | これ ですか。これ は | ストロベリー / ペパーミント / バナナ | です。

B | いくら ですか。

A | シングル は | 150円 / 200円 | です。ダブル は | 200円 / 300円 | です。

B | シングル / ダブル | は | たかい / やすい | ですね。 | ストロベリー / ペパーミント / バナナ | の | シングル / ダブル | を | 一つ / 二つ | ください。

A | 150円 / 200円 / 300円 / 400円 / 600円 | です。ありがとう ございます。

がんばれ

Accentuate the positive

Everyone learning Japanese, at one stage or another, gets a little bit discouraged by how hard it is to read the language. It can happen when a friend or family member asks you to read a brochure or a newspaper headline or sign, and you just can't do it.

But what these people may not realize is that for a Japanese learner, what comes first is speaking the language, a good practical skill that enables you to communicate with Japanese people. Whereas in, say, French or German, reading is perhaps the easiest language skill to acquire, in Japanese it is something requiring patient perseverance over a number of years. After all, it takes school students in Japan nine years to become familiar with all the characters in their own language!

This does not mean that you give up, of course. It just means that you have to be realistic and apply some positive reading skills to your Japanese reading. Let's take an example from the Disneyland survey in Unit 6.

パスポート が 4,000円、のこりの 5,000円 － 10,000円 が 食事代 と おみやげ代 に なります。

You will notice that in this sentence we have highlighted everything you know. You can read 'passport' in katakana, you know the kanji for yen (円) and for food (食), and you surely recognise the word おみやげ. You also know that this question is about how money was spent by students at Disneyland.

This is what you need to do every time you attempt to read something in Japanese. Don't focus on what you don't know, but highlight what you do. You will still be left with some gaps in your understanding, but you can often fill some of these with some intelligent guessing at the meaning from the overall context of the sentence. In this way you can often come to understand the gist of what you are reading.

So, accentuate the positive: think about the rapid progress you have made in speaking Japanese and, when it comes to reading, concentrate on what you do know.

うた・かぞえましょう

ペット は どうかぞえるの?
いっぴき、 にひき、 さんびき、 よんひきよ!
かぞえるの は やさしいよ!

ともだち は どうかぞえるの?
ひとり、 ふたり、 さんにん、 よにんよ!
かぞえるの は やさしいよ!

じしょ は どうかぞえるの?
いっさつ、 にさつ、 さんさつ、 よんさつよ!
かぞえるの は やさしいよ!

えんぴつ は どうかぞえるの?
いっぽん、 にほん、 さんぽん、 よんほんよ!
かぞえるの は やさしいよ!

りんご は どうかぞえるの?
ひとつ、 ふたつ、 みっつ、 よっつよ!
かぞえるの は やさしいよ!

いってみましょう

1 おみまい

You have probably heard how expensive some of the specially grown or imported fruit is in Japan. Below is a selection from a department store.

You and your friend are going to visit your teacher who is sick in hospital, and have decided to take some fruit. Take it in turns to point out what is available, how much it costs (whether or not it is expensive) and decide what you'll buy.

みかん
3kg **5,800**円

オレンジ
20コ **3,500**円

キーウィフルーツ
20コ **3,000**円

さくらんぼ
1kg **6,000**円

メロン
4,800円

パパイヤ
パパイヤ 4コ、レモン 1コ
3,500円

2 マクドナルド

You and your friend would both like to get a part-time job at マクドナルド on the ぎんざ during the summer holidays. You're both a bit worried about whether you'll be able to take down the orders and add up the prices quickly if the cash register breaks down.

Use the breakfast menu below to test each other. Take it in turns to decide what you'd like to have for breakfast and order it from your partner, who will take it down and tell you the total price.

You could take down the order in your own English (or Japanese!) shorthand, but you'll have to practise confirming the order and saying the prices in 日本語. Your order may sound like this:

ソーセージ マフィン を 一つ、ハッシュポテト を 二つ ください。そして ホット チョコレート を ください。

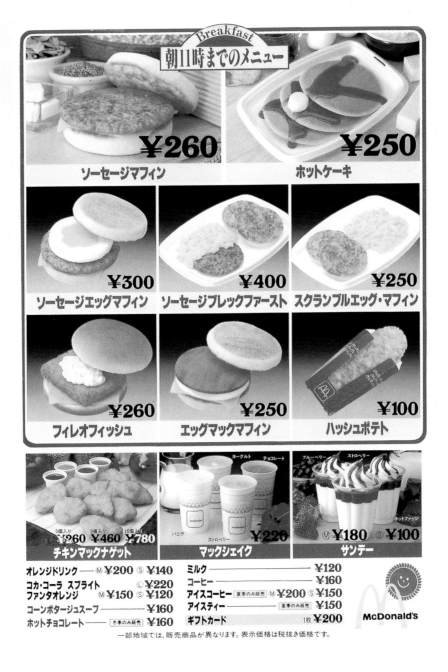

日本料理・Japanese food

If you visited Japan, you would find many familiar fast foods like スパゲッティ, ピザ and ハンバーガー, but why not try some *real* 日本料理.

すし is thin slices of raw fish resting on a small block of rice that has been flavoured with sweetened vinegar. This style of すし is called にぎりずし.

Beware of the わさび which is the very hot, green paste dabbed onto the rice. Can you guess why わさび has a nickname of なみだ (tears)?

Another popular style of すし is まきずし. This is strips of vegetables or fish placed on rice and rolled in のり seaweed. のり is dried seaweed which has been pressed into a crisp, flat, shiny sheet. The rolls are then cut into slices.

Another famous Japanese dish is てんぷら, which is a combination of pieces of fish and vegetables deep-fried in a very light batter. A dipping sauce with soy sauce, grated radish and ginger accompanies the dish. In some てんぷら restaurants in Japan, the てんぷら is cooked piece by piece in front of you and served to you immediately.

さしみ, like すし, is a raw fish dish. Slices of fresh fish are skilfully cut and arranged attractively. The slices are eaten after being dipped in soy sauce seasoned with わさび.

Accompanying these dishes and others may be soups such as みそしる or すいもの. みそしる is a soybean paste soup and many people enjoy it for breakfast. すいもの is a clear soup perhaps containing fish or chicken.

Of course Japan's staple food is rice (ごはん). The importance of rice is shown by the fact that the word ごはん means both *rice* and *a meal*. Steamed rice is served at nearly every meal. ごはん also is used as the base for a range of other dishes.

A quick lunch is てんどん which consists of deep-fried prawn cutlets on a bowlful of hot rice.

In Japan, the traditional 'fast food' has always been noodles. There are several kinds of noodles that are very popular. White うどん are made from wheat and are served piping hot in a soup, often with various accompaniments on top.

Brown そば noodles are made from buckwheat and these can also be served in a soup or they are tasty served with simply a dipping sauce.

Chinese noodles in 日本語 are called ラーメン and these are a popular dish to order in a Chinese restaurant or noodle shop.

All noodles are eaten with chopsticks and hearty slurping is not considered rude!

One-pot dishes cooked at the table are a regular family meal. The most famous of these is すきやき, a dish of thinly sliced meat, vegetables, とうふ (bean curd) and はるさめ (spring rain) noodles cooked together in a sweetened soy sauce broth.

Meals are completed with おちゃ, which is taken without milk or sugar.

日本語 ノート

一　Do you have . . .? Is there . . .?

In Unit 4 you learnt to use います to tell where people or animals are. To tell where things are, the verb あります is used. As with います, you must put に after the place.

e.g. パンや は あそこ に あります。
　　　The bakery is over there.
　　　うち は パンヤ の となり に あります。
　　　Our house is next door to the bakery.

As with (に)います, です can be used instead of (に)あります.

e.g. でんわ は つくえ の うえ です。
　　　The phone is on the desk.

あります is also used to mean *have*.

e.g. ピンク の マジック は ありますか。
　　　Have you got a pink highlighter pen?
　　　はい、あります。
　　　Yes, I have.
　　　いいえ、ありません。
　　　No, I haven't.

二　In between

To say something is between two things, you must name the two things on either side and then add (の)あいだ.

e.g. うち は がっこう と こうえん の あいだ です。
　　　Our house is in between the school and the park.

三　More about counting

You have learned to count your pets with the ひき counter for animals and to count friends and family with the り/にん (人) counter for people. There are many other counters used in 日本語. In some cases it depends on what is being counted. For example, if you want to count books, magazines etc., you must use さつ.

e.g. 本 を 三さつ 買いました。
　　　I bought three books.

In other cases it depends on the shape of the item. When you are counting long, thin objects like pens, pencils, trees, bottles etc., the counter ほん (本) is used.

e.g. えんぴつ を 六本 買いました。
　　　I bought six pencils.

Do note that you cannot count books (本) with the counter 本! さつ is counted in the same way as さい. To count one book is いっさつ, and eight books is はっさつ.

There is another number system that is used for things that do not clearly fit one of the 'counter' categories. These are the つ numbers.

e.g. ハンバーガー を 二つ 買いました。
　　　I bought two hamburgers.
　　　おかし を 八つ 食べました。
　　　I ate eight sweets.

The つ numbers, which only go to ten, are widely used. Little children often use ひとつ (一つ), ふたつ (二つ), みっつ (三つ) to tell their age. *Ten* in the つ numbers is written とお(十). In many Japanese advertisements you will notice that こ(コ) is often used to count small objects like pieces of fruit, eggs etc. The counters and つ numbers go *before* the verb or ください.

四　Using ください

In きもの 1, you learned to ask people to do things using ください.

e.g. ペン を かして ください。
　　　Please lend me your pen.

ください can also be used to ask for or to order things.

e.g. これ を ください。
　　　Please give me this.
　　　コーヒー を 二つ ください。
　　　Two coffees, please.

五　¥＝円

Japanese currency is called えん. In かんじ it is 円 and ¥ is the international symbol. 円 goes after the number (百円) but ¥ goes before (¥100).

単語

New words

あいだ — between
うえき — pot plant
うります — sell
くま — bear
たんす — wardrobe
となり — next to
にく — meat
もの — things

Expressions

いくら です か — How much is...?
いらっしゃいませ — welcome, can I help you?
しんじられない — that's unbelievable
しょうがない — can't be helped
ぜんぶで (いくらですか) — (How much) in all?

カタカナ の 単語

アンチック — antique
ガレージ セール — garage sale
ゴルフ クラブ — golf clubs
ゴルフ バッグ — golf bag
でんき スタンド — lamp
ポスト — post-box
マットレス — mattress
ランプ シェード — lampshade

Adjectives

すばらしい — wonderful
たかい — expensive, high
ふるい — old (for things)
りっぱ — great, magnificent
やすい — cheap

本や bookshop

~ さつ — counter for books
ざっし — magazine
じしょ — dictionary

ぶんぼうぐや stationery shop

はさみ — scissors
マジック — highlighter pen

やおや greengrocer

すいか — watermelon
みかん — mandarin
りんご — apple
やさい — vegetables

Numbers to 10 000

せん	1000
にせん	2000
さんぜん	3000
よんせん	4000
ごせん	5000
ろくせん	6000
ななせん	7000
はっせん	8000
きゅうせん	9000
いちまん	10 000

いくつ　　つ numbers

ひとつ	一つ	
ふたつ	二つ	
みっつ	三つ	
よっつ	四つ	
いつつ	五つ	
むっつ	六つ	
ななつ	七つ	
やっつ	八つ	
ここのつ	九つ	
とお	十	

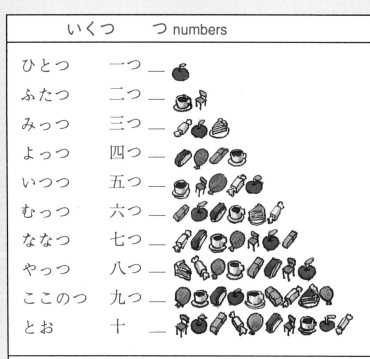

ココナツ を ここのつ ください。

はい。

なんぼん(何本)　本 counter

いっぽん	一本	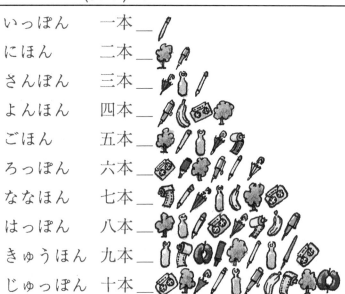
にほん	二本	
さんぼん	三本	
よんほん	四本	
ごほん	五本	
ろっぽん	六本	
ななほん	七本	
はっぽん	八本	
きゅうほん	九本	
じゅっぽん	十本	

おめでとう!

You are now able to use your 日本語 to:

- ask and tell where something is
- ask what is available when shopping
- ask and tell how much things cost
- decide what to buy
- calculate the price of items
- count various objects
- count to 10 000

第八課・はし が つかえますか。

みなさん、おはよう。

おはよう ございます。

きょう の じゅぎょう は...
さくぶん を かいて ください。

さくぶん!? ひどい!
せんせい、ビデオ
を 見ましょうよ。

だめ! さくぶん!

えんぴつ で かいて
も いいですか。

いいえ、くろい ペン
で かいて ください。

ローマじ で かいて も いいですか。

だめ ですよ。かんじ と
ひらがな と カタカナ で
かいて ください。だい は
「日本 へ 行きました。」
です。がんばって ね。

さくぶん　　なまえ: ホセ
「日本 へ 行きました」

　せんしゅう 日本 へ
行きました。
がいじん 日本一
コンテスト が
ありました。
...

がいこくじん 日本一
Japan's Number 1 Foreigner

ことしの がいじん
日本一 は ホセくん
です。おめでとう
ございます。

ホセくん、日本語 が
じょうず ですね。

ありがとう ございます。

すごい ですね。

おめでとう。

スピーチ! スピーチ。

ホセくん、何 を して
いますか。ここ に きて!

スピーチを...

何、これ!

さくぶん　　なまえ: ホセ
「日本 へ 行きました」

せんしゅう 日本 へ
行きました。
がいじん 日本一
コンテスト が
ありました。

みなさん、もう ひるやすみ
です。行って も いいですよ。

あれ?

いいましょう 一

nihon e ikimasu

Un voyage
au Japon

I'm going to Japan

我 到 日本去

Voy a Japon

日本 へ
行きます

ニホン へ
イキマス

Using the example as a guide, talk about which script or
language each character is using to write their essay.

例:

> A ゆうこさん は ひらがな で かいて いますか。
> B いいえ、カタカナ で かいて います。

いいましょう 二

スプーン

ナイフ

はし

て

フォーク

Using the example as a guide, say which implement
is best to use when eating these foods.

例:

| A てんぷら は て で 食べますか。 |
| B いいえ、はし で 食べます。 |

Using the example as a guide, talk about whether you are able to eat these foods.

例:

| A にく が 食べられますか。 |
| B はい、食べられます。 |
| or |
| いいえ、食べられません。 |

第八課 ● 百九

Using the example as a guide, ask if someone
is able to do these things or play these sports.
The verbs in the box may be of use.

例:

A かんじ が よめますか。
B はい、すこし よめます。
or
いいえ、あまり よめません。

A テニス が できますか。
B はい、できます。
or
いいえ、できません。

よめます
できます
かけます
つかえます

ともだちと

Aさん は 日本人 です。Bさんは がいこく人 です。
でんしゃの なか で はなしています。

Make up a conversation with a partner. Decide who will be A and who will be B.

A| ここ に すわって もいい ですか。

B| はい、どうぞ。

A| あ、日本語 が | はなせます / できます | ね。

B| すこし | はなせます。/ できます。 | 日本語 は | おもしろい / むずかしい | です。

A| ああ、そう ですか。 | ひらがな / カタカナ | は どうですか。 | かけますか。/ よめますか。

B| はい | かけます。/ よめます。 | がっこう で べんきょう しています。

A| がっこう で...? どこから きましたか。

B| アメリカ / オーストラリア / ニュージーランド | から きました。

A| ああ、そう ですか。せんせい は | 日本人 / アメリカ人 / ニュージーランド人 / オーストラリア人 | ですか。

B| はい、/ いいえ、 | 日本人 / アメリカ人 / ニュージーランド人 / オーストラリア人 | です。 | よく / いつも | 日本語 / えい語 | ではなします。

A| [B]さん / [B]くん | は 日本語 が じょうず ですね。

B| いいえ、そう でも ない です。

せいかつ

Hi everyone,

We're just back from this really excellent holiday. I just have to write about it before I forget all the details. I'll put it all in this letter, then I'll copy the best bits into my diary with my コピーペン.

Where do I start? Well, we went to 北海道. I suppose you've forgotten where it is. Have you got a map or something? It's an island and it's a really brilliant place. It's just so different from the rest of Japan. You know how, when you think of Japan, you think of ancient temples and traditions and crowded cities nearly all joining up, well, in 北海道 it's just the opposite. It's like Japan's wilderness area, just so natural and sort of untouched. It's all volcanoes and forests and stuff like that.

We nearly didn't get to see all of this. Mrs Tanaka's idea was to go to さっぽろ, the modern capital of 北海道 and spend two weeks in a luxury hotel there. It's a really modern city with everything well planned and it's really easy to find your way around to all the shops. She told Mr Tanaka about the big brewery there and said that we could all go and watch them making beer. That would be fascinating!

You might have heard of さっぽろ. It's where they had the 1972 Winter Olympics. It's also where they have the Snow Festival in February. The locals make these fantastic sculptures in ice and snow. I don't just mean snowmen, I mean full-sized replicas of buildings like the Opera House or huge monsters or giant slides. Here's one of シャーロック ホームズ.

The main reason there aren't that many cities on 北海道 is that it has really only been settled since 1868. Well, there were native people living there. They are called ainu, *and there are still some left, but not that many. We saw some of these Japanese aborigines in an ainu village. I suppose it was interesting, but I thought it was a bit sad because it was all touristy. They did this sort of native dance for us, but they didn't seem to have their hearts in it.*

I haven't been there in winter, but I have seen it all on TV. In February, all the channels here have daily news broadcasts with the latest from

the Snow Festival. About 2 million people go to the Snow Festival every year. I'm hoping to get there myself one year.

But I'm getting off the track, because we didn't really stay in さっぽろ and we didn't stay in a hotel, and we went in June. When we saw the holiday brochures about 北海道 and it being called キャンプロード, Toshio, Haruko and I wanted to go camping. It just seemed right to have a bit of a rugged holiday in this wild part of the world. The Tanakas didn't have any camping equipment, but you could hire everything you needed. I think it would have been really nice, with matching tent and camp furniture and sleeping bags and all that.

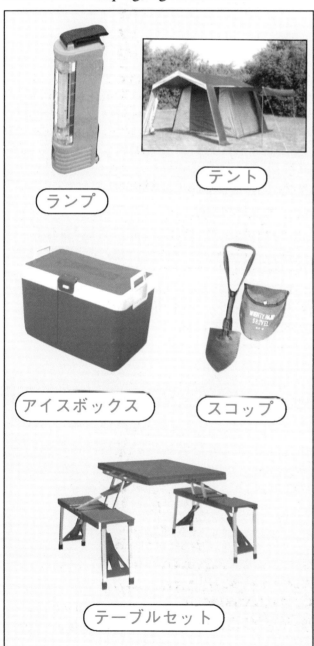

ランプ

テント

アイスボックス

スコップ

テーブルセット

But Mrs Tanaka was not in the mood for roughing it, and besides all Mr Tanaka could talk about was which campervan (キャンピングカー) we would choose. He kept telling Mrs Tanaka how luxurious they were, and when he spoke to us he said it was just like camping — except that we would have more room for video walkmans and computers and other essentials. I have to admit the camper we chose was really nice and I got to have the bed over the driver's cabin.

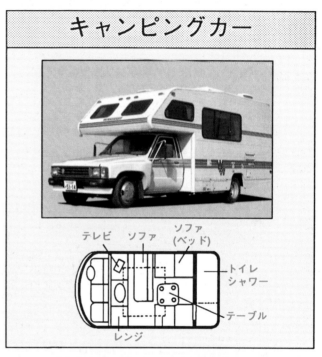

キャンピングカー

テレビ　ソファ　ソファ（ベッド）

トイレ
シャワー

テーブル

レンジ

We didn't pick up our campervan until we got to 北海道. To get there, we took the しんかんせん to the north of ほんしゅう, then we caught another train which took us under the sea to 北海道 through the Seikan Tunnel. This tunnel is 53 kilometres long and we were all looking forward to going through it. It was a bit disappointing, really, because you were going along, and then it just became dark and that was it. Still, I don't know what I expected. Half-way through the tunnel we got out and visited the museum they have there that shows you all this stuff about how they built it and that. It was finished in 1988.

The best part of our holiday in 北海道 was just being in such a wild place. It wasn't all tame and civilised, if you know what I mean. Mr Tanaka had to drive the campervan really carefully because there were all these really steep cliffs and volcanic craters and we kept thinking about going over. The most famous 北海道 volcano just popped up in a potato patch in 1945 while the farmer was working in it. It grew 20 cm a day for seven months and it erupted. After the eruption 北海道 had a new volcano, nearly 400 metres high. Lots of the volcanic craters on the island are filled up with beautiful lakes and you can walk around them or hire boats to go cruising on them. Then there were also lots of hot springs and steaming mud pools all over the island — no wonder there are so many おんせん in 北海道. The most famous one is called のぼりべつ おんせん. It's a huge complex of all different types of hot spa baths, all with luxury hotels around. I wasn't interested in the おんせん, but I was really rapt in じごく だに. Know what that means? The Valley of Hell. When you see it, you know why. It's this huge crater full of boiling mud. It has this scary, hissing sound and the smell is just disgusting — just like rotten egg gas. They say it is a favourite place for suicides. What an off place to jump into!

Summer in and around とうきょう can be really hot and humid, so a lot of Japanese people come to 北海道 where it is a lot cooler and drier. We saw lots of other campervans, especially in だいせつざん National Park, right in the centre of the island. If you can't go anywhere else in 北海道, go there. You can see all forests and waterfalls and that, as well as bears and deer. Well, we saw some deer, but we didn't see any bears until we went to this bear ranch. It was all right, but the bears seemed really bored and lazy.

The best animals we saw were the foxes at the fox shrine which was right near a peppermint farm. That's right, peppermint. You see it growing everywhere in the cleared areas outside the National Park and the plants look really excellent when they are in flower. I didn't know peppermint came from a plant. I thought it was just a flavour. Anyway, these foxes were really cute and friendly. They're my favourite animal now, they're just so foxy.

I should mention some of the food we had, too. My favourite thing was いしかり なべ, which is a sort of soup made up of chunks of salmon with vegetables, seaweed and みそ bean paste. Salmon is one of the most popular foods in 北海道. In fact, they really go in for all sorts of fish and seafood. In one place we saw けが に. These are great hairy crabs. They had giant replicas of them hanging over the doorway of the restaurant. It is illegal to catch these crabs, but it's not illegal to eat them. We didn't try them, we had ジンギスカン instead. It's a sort of lamb stew. The thing is, you know that all the ingredients are fresh in 北海道 because that's where many of the farms and fisheries are.

Anyway, it was a really great holiday. It was a part of Japan I didn't really know anything about. The people were really great, too. Living up there they didn't seem to be so worried about traditions and customs. It's hard to explain, but they seemed a bit freer or something. We were glad to get home, but now the Tanakas are talking about going back in February for the Snow Festival. That would be really fantastic. Mrs Tanaka might get her stay in her posh hotel.

I hope you can read these bits of brochures I've sent with the letter. It doesn't matter if you can't understand them all — I can't either. But you should get a good idea about a lot of it.

I'll be home in a few weeks and I'm looking forward to catching up with you all again. Until then,

Lots of love,

シモーン　　　より

日本語 ノート

一 More about で

You have learned that で means *by* a mode of transport.

e.g. バス で かえりました。
I came home by bus.

You have also used で to mean *at* (or *in*) a place.

e.g. みせ で 買いました。
I bought it at the shop.

で can also be used to mean *in* a language, or *in* a script such as ひらがな or ローマじ.

e.g. あの人 は フランス語 で はなして います。
He's speaking in French.
じゅうしょ を ローマじ で かいて ください。
Please write your address in romaji.

Yet another meaning of で is *with* an implement such as a pen or a knife.

e.g. はし で 食べました。
We ate with chopsticks.
えんぴつ で かいて は だめ です。
Don't write in pencil.

二 Can you do this?

To ask if someone can do a certain thing or to tell what you are able to do, a change is made to the verb. Look at the list below.

はいります	→	はいれます
つかいます	→	つかえます
まちます	→	まてます
かきます	→	かけます
あそびます	→	あそべます
よみます	→	よめます
はなします	→	はなせます

You have no doubt worked out that the い sound before ます is changing to an え sound, so り changes to れ, ち changes to て etc. The ひらがな chart also shows you what happens.

ま	み	む	め	も
ら	り	る	れ	ろ

Two groups of verbs are exceptions to this. One is the weak verb group.

食べます → 食べられます
おきます → おきられます

e.g. にく が 食べられますか。
Can you eat meat?

The other is the irregular verbs, where the verbs *do* or *play* and *come* change a lot.

きます → こられます
します → できます

e.g. あした こられますか。
Can you come tomorrow?
スポーツ が できますか。
Can you play sport?

The final thing you have to remember when using this form is to put が after the thing you can do.

e.g. かんじ が よめます。
I can read kanji.
カタカナ が かけます。
I can write katakana.

The question 日本語 が できますか is often asked of foreigners and while it means *Can you do Japanese?* it usually means *Can you speak Japanese?* You will, of course, be able to answer modestly はい、すこし できます。

三 Use of お

The sound お is often put in front of some words to give a more polite effect. This is done more frequently by female speakers. Many girls would say おはし for chopsticks. Boys could leave off the お in おはし in informal situations.

四 Use of へ

Like に, へ is also used to mean *to* a place. When it is used to mean *to* it is pronounced as *e*.

e.g. らいしゅう 日本 へ かえります。
I'm returning to Japan next week.

いってみましょう

1 ホーム・ステー

としおくん is coming to stay with your family for a week on a home-stay program. The Japanese school organising the visit has sent the profile below.

Your mother is becoming a little anxious about the visit. Your partner will take the part of your mother and ask you lots of questions about としおくん.

For example, she wants to know if he is used to animals, if he plays any sports and if he is interested in music. She is also concerned about whether or not he is able to speak or read English, what he can eat and what he can use to eat with.

Using the profile below, reassure your mother about としおくん's visit.

なまえ: いけだ としお

ねんれい:14

かぞく: 4人 (父、母、あね)

ペット:  ☑一ぴき  ☑二ひき

おんがく: ☑すき ☐ひけます ☑ひけます
☐きらい ☑ひけません ☐ひけません

スポーツ: ☑できます ☑できます
☐できません ☐できません

☐できます ☑できます
☑できません ☐できません

えいご: よめます ☑よく はなせます ☐よく
☐すこし ☑すこし

たべもの:きらいなもの: チーズ、トマト
すき なもの: にく、スパゲッティー、フルーツ

ナイフ と フォーク ☑つかえます
☐つかえません

2 ワープロ が つかえますか。

As supervisor of the zoo you have noticed that there are more and more Japanese bringing their children to see the animals. You've decided to hire someone to guide the children around and teach them about the animals in an entertaining way.

Certain skills are necessary for this special job. The person should like children and animals and be able to:

· speak Japanese
· write かんじ、ひらがな and カタカナ
· sing and play games
· use a word processor (for drawing up schedules etc.)
· come tomorrow

Draw up an interview sheet to record the details of each applicant (name, age, address, phone number) as well as their responses to your questions.

Interview three friends who will, of course, be very honest about their abilities, and decide who you will employ.

単語

New words	
がいこくじん (がいじん)	— foreigner
さくぶん	— essay
じゅぎょう	— lesson
だい	— title, topic
（お）はし	— chopsticks
ひるやすみ	— lunchtime

おめでとう

You are now able to use your 日本語 to:

· ask someone if they can do things
· tell someone what you can do
· explain what you use to eat with
· explain what language or script and what writing implement you use

Appendix
かんじ
(漢字)

人

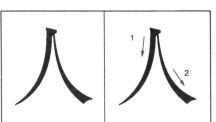

Meaning: *person*

Readings
ひと
じん、にん (り)

この人 (このひと)
日本人 (にほんじん)
三人 (さんにん)
二人 (ふたり)

月

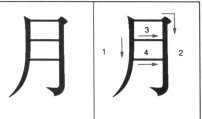

Meaning: *moon, month*

Readings

がつ、げつ

一月 (いちがつ)
四月 (しがつ)
今月 (こんげつ)
来月 (らいげつ)

日

Meaning: *sun, day*

Readings
ひ (び)
にち (に)

日本 (にほん)
日よう日 (にちようび)

本

Meaning: *origin, book*

Readings

ほん (ぽん、ぽん)

日本 (にほん)
本 (ほん)

語

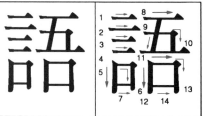

Meaning: *language*

Readings

ご

日本語 (にほんご)
単語 (たんご)
フランス語 (フランスご)

何

Meaning: *what?*

Readings
なに、なん

何語 (なにご)
何人 (なんにん)

母

Meaning: *mother*

Readings
はは
(お)かあ(さん)

母 (はは)
お母さん (おかあさん)

父

Meaning: *father*

Readings
ちち
(お)とう (さん)

父 (ちち)
お父さん (おとうさん)

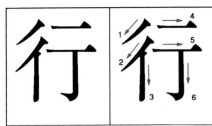

Meaning: *go*

Readings
い (きます)

行きます (いきます)
行って (いって)

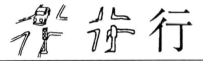

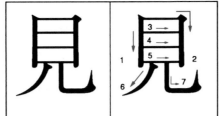

Meaning: *look, watch, see*

Readings
み (ます)

見ます (みます)
見て (みて)

Meaning: *eat*

Readings
た(べます)

食べます (たべます)
食べて (たべて)

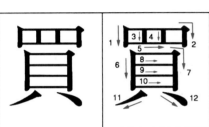

Meaning: *buy*

Readings
か (います)

買います (かいます)
買って (かって)

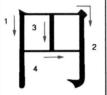

Meaning: *yen*

Readings

えん

百円 (ひゃく えん)
五円 (ごえん)

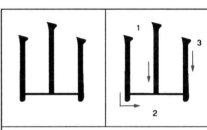

Meaning: *mountain*

Readings
やま

たかい 山 (たかい やま)

山

漢字 ● 百十九

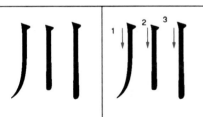

Meaning: *river*

Readings
かわ (がわ)

ながい 川 (ながい かわ)
山川さん (やまかわさん)

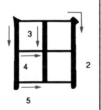

Meaning: *rice field*

Readings
た (だ)

山田 さん (やまださん)
本田さん (ほんださん)

単語・日本語ー英語

あ

アイス クリーム	ice-cream
あいだ	between
あおい	blue
あかい	red
あき	autumn
あさ	morning
あさごはん	breakfast
あし	leg, foot
あし の ゆび	toes
あそこ	over there
あそびます	play, muck about
あたたかい	warm
あたま	head
あびます	take (a shower)
あまり	not very, not often
あめ	rain
あらいます	wash
あります	there is (of things)

い

いい ですか	is that OK?
いいます	say
いかが ですか	how about this?
いくら ですか	how much?
いす	chair
いたい	it hurts
いつも	always
いっしょに	together
います	there is (of people, animals)
いや (な)	horrible, terrible
いらっしゃいませ	welcome
いろ	colour

う

うえ	on, above, up
うえき	pot plant
うしろ	behind
うそ	lie
うります	sell
うん	yes, yeah

え

え	picture
エアロビクス	aerobics
エレクトーン	electric organ
えん	yen (currency)

お

おきます	wake up, get up
おげんき です か	how are you?
おたく	your house
おなか	stomach, tummy
おなか が すいて (い)ます	I'm hungry
おねがい します	may I have?
おふろ	bath
おべんとう	boxed lunch
おみやげ	souvenir
おもしろい	interesting, fun
およぎます	swim
オレンジ ジュース	orange juice

か

か	or
カーテン	curtain
がいこくじん	foreigner
がいじん	foreigner
かえります	return
かお	face
かきます	write, draw
かっこいい	cool, spunky
かぜ	a cold
かみ(のけ)	hair
かめ	turtle
からだ	body

き

き	tree
きいろい	yellow
きせつ	season
ギター	guitar
きます	wear, put on
きょうしつ	classroom
きょねん	last year
きらい (な)	dislike
きれい (な)	pretty, clean
キロ (メートル)	kilo(metres)

く

くち	mouth
くつ	shoes
くま	bear
くもり	cloudy
クラブ	club
クレヨン	crayon
くろい	black

こ

こ、コ	counter for small objects

こ

こうてい	school ground
こうとうがっこう	senior high school
こうこう	senior high school
コーヒー	coffee
ここ	here
こどもたち	children
このひと	this person, he, she
ゴルフ	golf
こんでいます	crowded

さ

さかな	fish
さくぶん	essay
～さつ	counter for books etc.
ざっし	magazine
さむい	cold

し

ジーンズ	jeans
しけん	examination
じこしょうかい	self-introduction
じしょ	dictionary
しずか (な)	quiet
した	under, below, down
しゃしん	photograph
シャワー	shower
シャンプー	shampoo
しゅうまつ	weekend
じゅぎょう	lesson
しょうかい します	introduce
しょうがっこう	primary school
しょうが ない	can't be helped!
しろい	white
しんじられ ない	that's unbelievable
しんぶん	newspaper

す

すいか	water-melon
すずしい	cool
すてき (な)	nice, lovely
すばらしい	wonderful
スプーン	spoon
すんで います	live

せ

せ	height
せいと	student

せいふく	school uniform	ときどき	sometimes	ひきます	play a stringed
せん	thousand	とけい	watch, clock		instrument, catch
せんしゅ	player, athlete	とくい	good at		(a cold)
ぜんぜん	not at all	とても、とっても	very	ひくい	low
ぜんぶ	all, the lot	となり	next to	ひと	person
ぜんぶ で	in all	トライアスロン	triathlon	ひどい	dreadful
		とります	take	ひま	free

そ

		トレーニング	training	ひま なとき	spare time
そこ	there	どんな	what kind of?	びょういん	hospital
そして	and then			びょうき	sick, ill
それから	after that			ひるやすみ	lunchtime

な

		ナイフ	knife	ピンク (の)	pink

た

たいいくかん	gymnasium	なか	in		
たいかい	contest	ながい	long		
だい	title, topic	なつ	summer		

ふ

だいきらい	hate	なにいろ	what colour?	フォーク	fork
たいふう	typhoon	なにご (何語)	what language?	ぶた	pig
たかい	high, expensive	なまけもの	lazy thing	ふとりすぎ	too fat
たくさん	lots, many	なんにん (何人)	how many people?	ふります	fall (rain, snow)
たま に	occasionally	なんねんせい	what school level?	ふるい	old (things)
だめ	no good			~ふん	minutes
だれ	who?			ぶんぼうぐや	stationery shop
たんす	wardrobe				
ダンス	dance				

に

		にく	meat		

へ

				ベッド	bed

ち

ね

チャンピオン	champion	ねます	go to bed, sleep	ペット	pet
ちゅうがっこう	junior high school	~ねんせい	year level student	ベビー シッター	baby-sitter
ちゅうごく	China			へや	room
チョコレート	chocolate			へん (な)	strange
ちょっと	a bit			べんきょう します	study

の

		のち	later	ベンチ	park bench
		のど	throat		

つ

ほ

つかいます	use			ボールあそび	playing with a ball

は

つくえ	desk	はいります	enter, come in	ポスト	post box
つくります	make	はきます	put on, wear	ホットケーキ	pancake
つゆ	rainy season	はさみ	scissors	ホットドッグ	hot dog
		(お)はし	chopsticks	~ほん (本)	counter for long,
		はしります	run		thin objects

て

		はずかしかった	I'm embarrassed	ほんばこ	book case
て	hand	はな	flower, nose		
でかけます	go out	はなします	speak		

ま

てがみ	letter	はなみ	flower viewing	まい...	every...
できます	able to do	はやく	quickly, hurry up	まいにち	every day
でしょう	will be	はれ	fine weather	まえ	before, in front of
てんき	weather	パン	bread	マスク	(surgical) mask
でんき スタンド	lamp	ばんごはん	dinner, evening	マジック	highlighter pen
でんわ	telephone		meal	まん	ten thousand
		ハンサム (な)	good-looking,		
			handsome		

み

				みかん	mandarin (orange)

と

ひ

~ど	degrees			みせ	shop
	(temperature)	ピアノ	piano	みじかい	short
どうして	why?	~ひき	counter for small	みどり (の)	green
ドーナツ	doughnut		animals	みみ	ear
どうぶつ	animal				

め		
め		eye
も		
もう		already
もちろん		of course!
もの		thing
や		
～や		suffix indicating a shop
やおや		greengrocer
やさい		vegetable
やすい		cheap
やすみ		holiday
やめて		stop that!
ゆ		
ゆうめい（な）		famous
ゆき		snow
ゆび		finger
よ		
よい		good
よく		often
よく できました		well done
より		from (in a letter)
ら		
らいげつ		next month
り		
りっぱ（な）		great, magnificent
りんご		apple
れ		
れいぞうこ		refrigerator
ろ		
ロックコンサート		rock concert
わ		
わたし じゃない		not me
わたしたち		we

あさのかい
1 あさのあいさつ
2 あさのうた
3 けんこうかんさつ
4 みんなのはっぴょう
5 せんせいのおはな

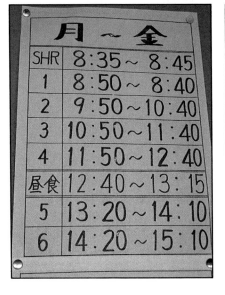

	月 ～ 金	
SHR	8:35 ～	8:45
1	8:50 ～	8:40
2	9:50 ～	10:40
3	10:50 ～	11:40
4	11:50 ～	12:40
昼食	12:40 ～	13:15
5	13:20 ～	14:10
6	14:20 ～	15:10

3-2 時間割

＼	月	火	水	木	金	土
1	英	日	英	現	古	数
2	数	数	日	生	日	日
3	古	選	化	日	選	現
4	体	英C	体	化	数	化
5	現	英	数	英C	英	
6	化	生	LHR	体	クラブ	

単語・英語―日本語

A

above	うえ
aerobics	エアロビクス
all, the lot	ぜんぶ
already	もう
animal	どうぶつ
apple	りんご
athlete	せんしゅ
autumn	あき

B

bakery	パンや
bath	おふろ
take a bath	おふろに はいります
bear	くま
bed	ベッド
go to bed	ねます
before	まえ
behind	うしろ
below	した
between	あいだ
a bit	ちょっと
black	くろい、ブラック
blue	あおい、ブルー
body	からだ
bookcase	ほんばこ
bread	パン
breakfast	あさごはん

C

chair	いす
cheap	やすい
children	こども、こどもたち
China	ちゅうごく
chopsticks	（お）はし
classroom	きょうしつ
clean	きれい（な）
clock	とけい
cloudy	くもり
cold	さむい
(a) cold	かぜ
have a cold	かぜを ひいて います
colour	いろ
come in, enter	はいります
contest	たいかい
cool	すずしい
cool (spunky)	かっこいい
counters	
for animals	ひき
for books	さつ
for long, thin objects	本
for small objects	こ、つ
crowded	こんで います

D

desk	つくえ
dictionary	じしょ
dinner	ばんごはん
dislike	きらい（な）
down	した
draw	かきます
dreadful	ひどい

E

ear	みみ
electric organ	エレクトーン
enter, come in	はいります
essay	さくぶん
everyday	まいにち
examination	しけん
expensive	たかい
eye	め

F

face	かお
famous	ゆうめい（な）
finger	ゆび
fish	さかな
flower	はな
flower viewing	はなみ
foot	あし
foreigner	がいこくじん、がいじん
free time	ひま なとき
fridge	れいぞうこ
fun	おもしろい

G

get up	おきます
good	よい、いい
go out	でかけます
green	みどり（の）、グリーン
greengrocer	やおや
guitar	ギター
gymnasium	たいいくかん

H

hair	かみ（のけ）
hand	て
handsome	ハンサム（な）
hate	だいきらい
head	あたま
height	せ
high	たかい
holiday	やすみ
horrible	いや（な）
hospital	びょういん
how many people?	なんにん(何人)
how much?	いくら
hungry	おなかが すいて（い）ます
(it) hurts	いたい

I

ice-cream	アイスクリーム
ill	びょうき
in	なか
interesting	おもしろい
introduce	しょうかいします
introduce oneself	じこ しょうかい

J

| jeans | ジーンズ |

L

leg	あし
letter	てがみ
lie	うそ
live	すんで います
long	ながい
lots	たくさん
low	ひくい
lunch (boxed)	おべんとう
lunchtime	ひるやすみ

M

magazine	ざっし
magnificent	りっぱ（な）
make	つくります
mandarin (orange)	みかん
many	たくさん
meat	にく
morning	あさ
mouth	くち

N

newspaper	しんぶん
next to	となり
nice	すてき（な）

nose	はな	scissors	はさみ	wash	あらいます
not much, very	あまり	season	きせつ	watch	とけい
		sell	うります	water-melon	すいか
O		shoes	くつ	we	わたしたち
occasionally	たま に	shop	みせ	wear	
often	よく	short	せ が ひくい	lower part of body	はきます
old	ふるい	shower	シャワー	top part of body	きます
on	うえ	take a shower	シャワー を	weather	てんき
or	か		あびます	cloudy	くもり
over there	あそこ	sick	びょうき	fine	はれ
		snow	ゆき	welcome	いらっしゃいませ
P		it snows	ゆき が ふります	what?	なん、なに(何)
person	ひと (人)	sometimes	ときどき	colour?	なにいろ
pet	ペット	sore	いたい	kind of?	どんな
keep pets	ペット を かって	souvenir	おみやげ	language?	なにご(何語)
	います	speak	はなします	school year?	なんねんせい
photograph	しゃしん	spunky	かっこいい	white	しろい、ホワイト
picture	え	stationery shop	ぶんぼうぐや	who?	だれ
pig	ぶた	stomach	おなか	why?	どうして
play about	あそびます	strange	へん (な)	wonderful	すばらしい
play a keyboard		student	せいと	write	かきます
or stringed		study	べんきょう		
instrument	ひきます		します		
play a sport	します	summer	なつ	**Y**	
player	せんしゅ	swim	およぎます	yeah, yes	うん
post box	ポスト			year	
pot plant	うえき	**T**		last year	きょねん
pretty	きれい (な)	take	とります	yellow	きいろい、
put on		tall	せ が たかい		イエロー
lower part of body	はきます	telephone	でんわ	yen	えん、(円)
top part of body	きます	terrible	いや (な)		
		there	そこ		
Q		thing	もの		
quickly	はやく	thousand	せん		
quiet	しずか (な)	throat	のど		
		title	だい		
R		toes	あし の ゆび		
rain	あめ	together	いっしょに		
it rains	あめ が ふります	tree	き		
rainy season	つゆ	turtle	かめ		
red	あかい、レッド	typhoon	たいふう		
refrigerator, fridge	れいぞうこ				
return	かえります	**U**			
room	へや	under	した		
run	はしります	up	うえ		
		use	つかいます		
S					
say	いいます	**V**			
school		vegetable	やさい		
ground	こうてい	very	とても、とっても		
junior high	ちゅうがっこう				
primary	しょうがっこう	**W**			
senior high	こうとうがっこう	wake up	おきます		
	(こうこう)	wardrobe	たんす		
uniform	せいふく	warm	あたたかい		

単語 ● 百二十四

throwing
pottery masterclass

throwing

pottery masterclass

practical techniques

for modern ceramics

Josie Warshaw
Richard Phethean

Photography by Stephen Brayne

southwater

To Ronald and Sylvia,
Peter and Clem, with thanks and love.

This edition is published by Southwater

Southwater is an imprint of
Anness Publishing Limited
Hermes House
88-89 Blackfriars Road
London
SE1 8HA
tel. 020 7401 2077
fax 020 7633 9499

Distributed in the USA by
Anness Publishing Inc.
27 West 20th Street
Suite 504
New York, NY 10011
tel. 212 807 6739
fax 212 807 6813

Distributed in the UK by
The Manning Partnership
251-253 London Road East
Batheaston
Bath
BA1 7RL
tel. 01225 852 727
fax 01225 852 852

Distributed in Australia by
Sandstone Publishing
Unit 1, 360 Norton Street
Leichhardt
New South Wales 2040
tel. 02 9560 7888
fax 02 9560 7488

© 2000
Anness Publishing Limited

10 9 8 7 6 5 4 3 2 1

Publisher: Joanna Lorenz
Project editor: Emma Clegg
Assistant editor: Martin Goldring
Consultant advisor: John Forde
US advisor: Nancy Selvage
Copy editor:
  Samantha Ward-Dutton
Projects copy editor:
  Gail Dixon-Smith
Reader: Joy Wotton
Designer: Celia Clay
Photographer: Stephen Brayne
Stylist: Diana Civil
Picture researcher:
  Pernilla Pearce
Illustrator: Robert Highton
Production controller:
  Don Campaniello

Previously published as part of a
larger compendium,
The Complete Practical Potter

NOTES

Learning a new craft can be tremendous fun, filling many
rewarding hours, but certain materials and equipment may need
to be handled with great care. The author and publishers have
made every effort to ensure that all the instructions in this book
are accurate and safe, but cannot accept liability for any resultant
injury, damage or loss to persons or property, however it
may arise.

Designed for an international readership, terms are occasionally
bracketed to clarify the different specialist and general terms.
To avoid confusion, note that the first firing stage in the UK is
"biscuit firing", whereas the US refer to this as "bisque firing".
Also that the UK use an additional term "bisque" to mean a
particular firing that has a higher temperature than the
glaze firing that follows.

Captions for photographs of final work give the measurements
of the piece by height, unless otherwise specified.

PICTURE CREDITS

Josie Warshaw, Sabina Teuteberg, Jennifer Lee, Peter Lane, John
Dawson, Sue Paraskeva, Kyra Cane, Prue Venables, Lucie Rie,
Hans Coper, Fenella Mallalieu, Mike Dodd, Jane Hamlyn, Ashley
Howard, Neil Tetkowski, Colin Pearson, Aki Moriuchi, Keith
Ashley, Emmanuel Cooper, Howard Shooter, Jenny Beavan,
Sandy Brown, Jane Hamlyn, Kate Malone, Margaret Forde, Jeff
Oestreich and Jane Perryman.

The editors would also like to thank all those who contributed
projects for use in the book: Nick Arroyave-Portela (Undulating
Vase), 41 Delancey Street, London NW1 7RX; Chris Bramble
(Three-footed Bowl), 25 Kingsgate Workshops, 110-116
Kingsgate Road, London NW6 2JG; Nick Membery (Oval Baking
Bowl), 8 Culford Mews, 157 Balls Pond Road, Hackney, London
N1 4BG; Sue Paraskeva (Porcelain Bowl), 70 Mountgrove Road,
Arsenal, London N5 2LT; Richard Phethean (Cup and Saucer,
Teapot, Jug, Sectional Vase and Wide-rimmed Dish), The
Leadenporch House, New Street, Deddington, Banbury, Oxon
OX15 0SP.

CONTENTS

INTRODUCTION

Like many of my generation I came to clay initially through the influence of the Leach tradition. Bernard Leach's philosophy combined Eastern and Western ideas and was highly influential in shaping and building the studio pottery movement. He set a code of pottery practice that related both to the use of materials and to an appropriate pottery aesthetic. During formative years my attraction to clay was associated with the conventional ideas of the time about the material.

Working with clay seemed then to be accompanied by a resistance to the modern world of the synthetic or the mass produced. For myself, as an impressionable adolescent, my first clay mentor had an aura of oriental mysticism and accompanying spirituality. There was the seduction of the feel of the clay and the fascination of the processes – watching shapes take form on the wheel and seeing how the firing process transformed the colour and glaze. I found wood, oil, raku and gas firing particularly exciting, and could hardly wait for the tantalizing moment when the door of the kiln opened. To this day I still become excited when the temperature creeps low enough to ease open the door and take a peek inside. In time, this fascination turned into understanding, but the challenge to explore, to invent and to express myself in my ceramic work continues.

Many of you may just be starting to work with ceramics and will be bringing with you fresh thinking and original creative approaches. This ensures that design and techniques are continually being injected with new ideas, unhindered by the often restricting oriental approach of Leach. The history of ceramics shows that the main processes and techniques have not changed, but that creative design has moved on. With hindsight we can see that it is the ideas of a particular period or culture that makes each historical development distinctive and recognizable, and that current thinking is central to how ceramics is valued and appreciated. In today's climate the choices are open and the contemporary maker is relatively free to interpret and explore ideas of aesthetics, subject, culture and materials in a personal way.

In recognition of this freedom Richard Phethean and I have tried to accommodate a wide range of technical possibilities and have presented methods of working with clay both for the beginner and for the more experienced maker, using clay as a medium for functional craftwork as well as for other more artistic purposes, such as thrown sculptural to architectural work.

LEARNING TO WALK BY J WARSHAW, 1996.

Throwing is often misconceived as the only method that is applied to functional ceramics. There are however the other major technique areas of handbuilding and mouldmaking both of which can be used not only on their own but also in conjunction with the technique of throwing. The other common but mistaken perception regarding throwing is that it is a technique used solely to produce functional domestic items. There are now many examples of contemporary work which use the same techniques described in these pages to make sculptural to architectural items. Though this book contains descriptions of a number of the more central techniques to do with glazing, decoration and firing, the great creative potential within their scope should also not be underestimated. For example, particularly suitable for thrown domestic ware purposes and often dismissed or unrecognized, one of those described is the use of single firing which enables continuity and economy in the working method and a more spontaneous movement from making through to final glazing.

Richard and I hope that this book will serve as a practical, approachable and comprehensive manual for the beginner as well as providing inspiring insights into the more advanced techniques of throwing.

CLAY: THE FUNDAMENTAL INGREDIENT

An abundant natural material, clay forms primarily around large granite outcrops, but is found all around us, in gardens, fields, and along riverbanks or roadsides. It contains alumina and silica, as well as small quantities of other minerals, and originates from feldspathic or granite rock, originally molten when the earth was formed, and transformed over millions of years by decomposition and weathering. Different proportions of the main and subsidiary minerals give each clay its individual qualities.

Primary and secondary clays

There are two geological categories of clay: primary and secondary clays. Primary clays, which are found where they originally formed, include china clay or kaolin, a very pure clay used to give strength and whiteness to porcelain. Another is bentonite, which can be added to other clay to improve the plasticity of clay bodies. Secondary clays were deposited in sedimentary layers during their formation. Examples are ball clays, often blue or black in their unfired state, which also add plasticity and become white or buff after firing, and red clays that contain iron oxide, which acts as a flux that lowers the clay's firing temperature. This clay is used to make earthenware bricks, floor tiles and flowerpots.

Altering a clay body

Materials can be added to a clay body to change and strengthen it. Altering a clay body in this way reduces the shrinkage rate and lessens the degree of stress during drying and firing.

You can mix clays at the dry or plastic stage to bring them to a required state of workability or openness and modify the colour and texture at the same time. Grog is a common material that is used to 'open' clay. It is a pre-fired clay that has been ground and prepared to different graded particle sizes ranging from dust to grit. You can add grogs to any clay to make it suitable for raku firing (see kiln firing, raku firing), enabling the clay to withstand the thermal shock of dramatic temperature change. Grog will also bleed through a glaze at high temperatures to give a speckled effect. Ovenware clay bodies are designed with the addition of clay 'openers' such as lithium feldspar or talc in a silica-free body.

Other materials used to change a clay body include molochite, quartz, sand or fibrous material such as paper.

Obtaining clay

Clay can be dug from the ground and prepared by slaking (see reclaiming clay), sieving and returning it to its plastic state. It is marginally easier to buy clay in dry, powdered individual materials which can then be mixed together. Both methods are labour-intensive and, in the case of preparing clay from dry materials, you will need to have access to specialist equipment.

Alternatively, it is possible to buy ready-made clay in a plastic state, packaged in sealed polythene bags, from a ceramic supplier. As you will also need to pay for the cost of delivery, then the more clay you buy the cheaper it will be per unit of weight. You can also buy or prepare different clays in a liquid state, called casting slip, for slip casting (a forming technique of pouring clay into plaster moulds).

Choosing a clay

Each clay has its own distinct make-up, resulting in a different handling quality, colour, temperature range and plasticity, or workability. These qualities are specified by ceramic suppliers and many will be willing to send small sample bags of clay through the post for you to test. The choice of clays is wide and you can also combine them, which will increase the possibilities further. Ready-prepared clays can be combined by weighing out the selected proportions of each clay and wedging and kneading them until thoroughly mixed (see preparing clay).

There are many things that you should find out about a clay that you are considering using. First of all, test its plasticity (see plasticity test). You should also establish whether a clay is suited to oxidized or reduced firing, if it is appropriate for your planned working methods, and what is its texture and fired colour, as well as its price. Most clays are suitable for any making technique, but there are some that are specifically designed for certain ones. A very plastic clay body designed and developed specifically for throwing purposes, for example, might not be suitable for the task of modelling fine detail where a smooth fine-particle clay will be more effective. If the correct clay is not selected, then you might find the forming clay stage to be a struggle, or encounter problems with the drying and firing processes.

Remember that changes can be made to the colour or texture of clay, as well as to its actual physical properties – namely its plasticity, workability and shrinkage rate. Alternatively, changes might be made to the clay body by either raising or lowering the degree of heat necessary in the kiln to achieve the required fired density.

The list of available clays is wide, though in practice dependent upon the ceramic supplier you use and the range they have on offer.

Throwing clays

These are dense, plastic and responsive. To increase the plasticity of a clay for throwing, up to 30 per cent ball clay is added (more than this will cause shrinkage and drying problems and also make the clay sticky). To give throwing clay extra staying power when standing on the wheel after being intensively worked, add up to 10 per cent grog or coarse clay at a particle size that will pass through a 30–60 mesh.

Handbuilding and modelling clays

These tend to be open clays to enable limited shrinkage and safe drying and firing, combined with adequate plasticity. A coarse or fine grog, or silver-sand addition can be introduced into a smooth clay body – depending on the texture that you require, add up to 20–30 per cent to prepare a clay in this way.

T-material is a handbuilding clay (only available in the UK) with a plastic coarse texture that fires to a white or off-white colour. Its specially developed formula means that it is plastic to work with and has a low shrinkage rate, so does not warp or distort.

Fibrous or paper clay

This is any clay to which fibres have been introduced. The raw clay is very strong, giving extra stability to fragile constructions. It is also easy to dry and to mend if broken or cracked.

Casting clays

These clays must deflocculate, or break up into fine particles, to create casting slips. Clays that contain a large amount of iron or free alkali do not deflocculate and are not suitable for casting. The purer clays such as kaolin and ball clay, many buff burning stoneware clays and fire clay deflocculate and therefore cast well. A body that casts well is usually not plastic enough for throwing.

Jigger and jolley clays

These clays are designed for use with the jigger and jolley technique. This technique involves the use of accurately made and centered plaster moulds placed and held by a cup wheel head, which revolves like a thrower's wheel. They need to have moderate plasticity and should dry with a minimum of shrinkage and warpage.

Plasticity test

If you need to add grog or sand into plastic clay to reduce its shrinkage rate, you can calculate how much to add by weight or volume. To test how much grog can be kneaded into clay without losing its plasticity roll out a coil of clay to a width of about 2 cm (¾ in) and bend it to form a ring. If the clay cracks, it is 'short' and will be difficult to work. You can also measure plasticity by noting the

amount of water you need to add to a measured amount of dry clay to take it to a suitable consistency. A finer clay requires more water than an open clay. If a clay contains more water, it will subsequently shrink more.

The clay temperature range

Clay can be subdivided into five various temperature range groups:

- Earthenware has a maturing range of 1000–1180°C (1832–2156°F).

- Stoneware has a maturing range of 1200–1300°C (2192–2372°F).

- Porcelain has a maturing range of 1240–1350°C (2264–2462°F).

- Bone china has a maturing range of 1240–1250°C (2264–2282°F).

- Coloured clay has a maturing range of 1040–1220°C (1904–2228°F).

Earthenware

Fired earthenware has a much lighter feel to higher fired clays, which have a more compact, dense quality. The colour of earthenware ranges from grey or white, to red, orange, buff, yellow and brown. Earthernware clay is abundant and available in nearly every part of the world. Red clay is a secondary clay found near the surface of the ground, which contains iron oxide, accounting for its relatively low firing temperature. Red clay is usually plastic and therefore suitable for modelling, building and pressing as well as for throwing. Light or white

earthenware bodies are made by blending light burning clays, such as ball clay and china clay, or a stoneware clay with fluxes, such as talc frit or nepheline syenite, to give sufficient plasticity.

Stoneware

The name "stoneware" comes from the dense, hard character of the clay body. The colour range for stoneware includes off-white, tan, grey and brown. Fired stoneware clay that is fully matured or vitrified has a water absorption rate of 3 per cent or less. The higher firing temperature of this clay means that adding a flux is less necessary. However this high temperature also means that feldspar can be used as a flux (as a 10–20 per cent addition) whenever necessary in order to lower the maturing temperature.

Porcelain

The word "porcelain" is said to have evolved from "porcellno", a descriptive word given by Marco Polo in the 13th century to a translucent cowrie shell that looked like a little pig. This white-firing vitreous clay is translucent if worked to a thin wall and is fired to temperatures of 1240°C (2264°F) and above. It is made by combining white burning clays with feldspars and flint. The high firing temperature causes the particles to become dense and impervious and gives fired porcelain similar qualities to glass. The ball clays, china clays or kaolin used

EGYPTIAN DIARY
(32 x 7.5 CM / 12½ X 3 IN)
CLAY COLLAGE WALL PIECE, THIN PIECES OF COLOURED
CLAY ARE LAID ON TOP OF THE BASE SLAB
(SABINA TEUTEBERG).

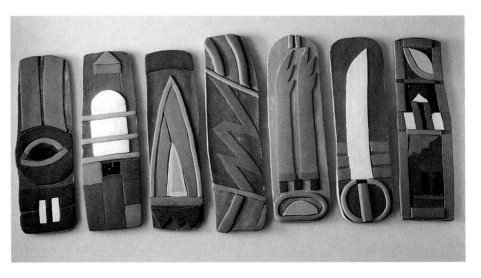

CLOCKWISE FROM TOP LEFT: PLASTIC CLAY FOR BONE CHINA, COLOURED CLAY, PORCELAIN, STONEWARE AND EARTHENWARE.

in porcelain must be iron free and as plastic as possible. It is difficult to develop a porcelain for throwing, as the majority of white clays are characteristically non-plastic.

Bone china

This porcelain clay is made from calcined ox bones, and is produced mainly in England and Japan. It was developed in the 18th century to meet the demand for a white translucent ware to compete with imported oriental porcelain. The clay body is difficult to work, being very short when plastic and fragile when dry. It is most suitable for slip casting, but with the addition of up to 6 per cent bentonite can also be press moulded.

Glaze firing is at a low temperature of 1080–1100°C (1976–2072°F).

Coloured clay

Any clay can be coloured with oxide or stain additions, although a light or white coloured clay will give the best colour response. Adding colour will often lower a clay's firing temperature, so tests should be carried out.

Maturing temperatures

Clay is often referred to as "maturing" or "vitrifying" at a certain temperature. This is the point at which a body reaches its maximum fired strength and compactness, resulting from its progressive fusion during firing. Below this temperature the

body is underfired, and will be weak and porous. Conversely, if a clay body is fired beyond its maturing temperature range then a number of faults can also occur, such as warping, bloating, collapsing or eventual transformation to a molten state. In the case of porcelain and bone china a state of near complete fusion is obtained resulting in their translucent qualities.

Research and consider carefully before selecting a clay – it should not only be suitable for your working method, but also have a temperature range to suit the glaze and the firing. Consider this when you are designing the format, scale, finished surface and the overall "feel" of the piece.

Clay shrinkage

One aspect of clay not always detailed in a supplier's catalogue is its shrinkage rate. Clays shrink at an approximate rate of 10–13 per cent from their raw to fired state, the highest shrinkage rate taking place from the leatherhard to the bone dry state. A higher shrinkage rate is very difficult to work with, so a fine-particle, dense clay can be "opened up" by adding materials, such as sand or grog (see preparing clay, kneading in additions) to reduce shrinkage. However, the grain structure of a clay is closely related to its plasticity or workability – the more open a clay, the less plastic it will become – so take care not to add too much grog.

Clays that are very dense can pose problems when attaching clay to clay, as in the case of joining handles (or slab building). The high shrinkage rate increases the chances of cracks forming at joints during drying and firing. Surfaces you wish to remain flat can also warp or curl at the edges when dried and/or fired. Slow drying by wrapping the work in plastic and slow firing can get around some of the problems, but if this does not work, you will need to rethink your design or experiment with the composition of the clay body.

Shrinkage test

Any clay body with or without added grog or other openers can be tested for shrinkage using the following method:

1 Roll out a sheet of plastic clay approximately 1 x 2 cm (½ x ¾ in) thick and cut it into three strips about 14 x 4 cm (5½ x 1½ in).

2 Accurately mark a line 10 cm (4 in) long with a sharp knife point and leave the strips to dry.

3 Turn them frequently to avoid warping.

4 Measure the length of the lines when the clay strips are bone dry.

5 Fire the test pieces to their intended maturing temperature and measure the length of the lines of shrinkage again. If the final shrinkage rate from plastic to fired exceeds 10–13 per cent, i.e. if the line ends up at 9 cm (3½ in) or less, the clay body will be difficult to use and you will need to add grog (see preparing clay, kneading in additions).

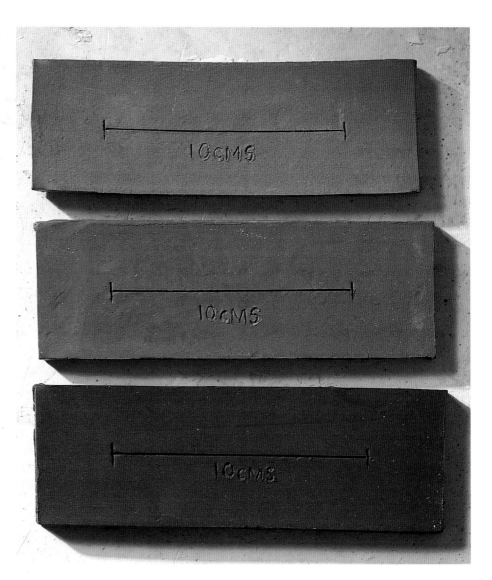

THE PHOTOGRAPH ABOVE SHOWS THE SHRINKAGE TEST RESULTS FOR FIRED EARTHENWARE (TOP), DRY EARTHENWARE (MIDDLE) AND PLASTIC EARTHENWARE (BOTTOM). THE LINES MARKED ON THE PLASTIC CLAY ARE 10 CM (4 IN) LONG AND ARE MEASURED AFTER FIRING TO RECORD SHRINKAGE RATES.

CALCULATING PERCENTAGE LINEAR SHRINKAGE

The following equations give the method of calculating shrinkage rates from plastic to dry, dry to fired and plastic to fired clay.

$$\% \text{ DRY SHRINKAGE (plastic to dry)} = \frac{\text{Plastic length} - \text{dry length}}{\text{Plastic length}} \times 100$$

$$\% \text{ FIRED SHRINKAGE (dry to fired)} = \frac{\text{Dry length} - \text{fired length}}{\text{Dry length}} \times 100$$

$$\% \text{ TOTAL SHRINKAGE (plastic to fired)} = \frac{\text{Plastic length} - \text{fired length}}{\text{Plastic length}} \times 100$$

Fired maturity test

In some instances, such as if you are planning a piece of work that must resist taking in water to prevent frost damage, you will need to establish whether a clay has reached its fired maturity or full vitrification. To test the degree of water absorption on fired clay, weigh and mark for indentification three clay bars, which have been fired at the required temperatures to be tested. Boil them in water for two hours and weigh them again. Compare their weights – if there is no change, no water has been absorbed and the fired clay will be fully vitrified.

Consistency

The consistency of a clay will affect the limits of the work to be made. A firmer clay will stand longer working time on the wheel or allow a higher wall to be built from joined coils. If additional elements are made from softer clay, this will allow a coil or handle to be attached with less pressure to a supporting form or a turned lid.

Clay should be soft enough to move but firm enough so that it does not stick to hands and surfaces. It does not take long to acquire a feel for the correct "give" and to assess the best consistency for using clay for the particular job in hand. If it is a struggle in either direction, wedge either softer or firmer clay, depending on which way the clay needs to go, into the mass.

Clay that is too wet can be kneaded on dry plaster slabs (see preparing clay) until enough moisture has been extracted and the clay is in a usable plastic state. If your clay is too firm and you have no spare soft clay, the only option is to leave the clay to go dry for reclaiming. You can save clay that is verging on being too firm to use by making holes in its mass, pouring in water, letting it soak in and then wedging the clay. Alternatively, you can leave the clay to soak and soften in a container of water.

Clay storage

Clay can be stored for long periods of time in airtight plastic bags. If the bags get torn, seal them with strong plastic tape to prevent air reaching the clay. Clay can also be stored in airtight containers. For shorter storage periods wrap clay in sheets of plastic to prevent it from drying out. You can also use this system to store and retain work at the leatherhard stage.

Using clay within the projects

The type of clay used In each of the projects is always specified and suitable alternatives are given. Weights of clay are given for some of the projects, although the exact quantity needed will depend on the scale and volume of work you are making. Remember that unused clay will keep for long periods as long as it is stored in airtight polythene or plastic.

WHITE GARDEN (14 CM/5½ IN)
PORCELAIN, WHEEL THROWN, PAINTED WITH ACRYLIC
RESIST AND SUCCESSIVE LAYERS SPONGED AWAY, FIRED
UNGLAZED IN A REDUCING ATMOSPHERE (PETER LANE).

DARK POT WITH SLATE BLUE RIM (15.5 CM/6 IN)
T-MATERIAL COLOURED WITH OXIDES, PINCHED,
COILED AND OXIDIZED (JENNIFER LEE).

EQUIPMENT
PREPARING CLAY Bought clay needs to go through the initial preparation processes of

wedging and kneading, or alternatively pugging, before being ready to work with. In addition to this, and

because about one third of plastic clay is water and clay delivery is paid for by weight, many makers who work

with large quantities find it economical to make their own clay using dry materials or by refining local clay.

For large quantities
A large clay blunger is used in
combination with a filter press for preparing
large amounts of plastic clay. It contains a
rotating vertical shaft with mounted paddles
or blades. The dry materials are weighed
then mixed with water in the blunger and
passed through a vibrating sieve into a filter
or clay press. This squeezes the water out of
the liquid clay using pressure. The slabs of
freshly made plastic clay are then peeled
away from the cloths in the press to be
stored or pugged ready for use.

An electric clay mixer is also used for
preparing large quantities of clay, blending
500–750 kg (1000–1500 lbs) of dry materials
into a clay body at a time. The materials are
measured and added to the water in the
mixer. This rotates and blends them to a
plastic workable consistency.

A small blunger (shown above) is used
for mixing clay with water so as to prepare
liquid casting slips for use in techniques such
as slip casting.

A pugmill is a metal barrel or cylinder,
tapered at one end to a die. Clay is forced
through the die by a rotating screw that
consolidates and homogenizes the clay as it
passes through. Clay that has been pugged
can be used without wedging and kneading,
as long as it is used immediately.

For small quantities
If you are preparing smaller quantities of clay,
then you will need the following equipment:

1   A fixed bench made from a heavy
material, such as a concrete paving stone or
slate. Ensure it is at a comfortable height to
be wedged roughly as high as the top of
your thigh.

2   A dry plaster slab (bat) used for
reconstituting wet clay can be simply made
with potter's casting plaster. Damage to
plaster slabs should be avoided as plaster
contaminates clay.

3   Scales and weights are also needed to
weigh prepared clay into equal-sized balls.

4   A flat-headed paint scraper to clear any
surplus clay on the bench (not shown).

5   Cutting wire for cutting the clay.

6   Plastic for storing prepared clay.

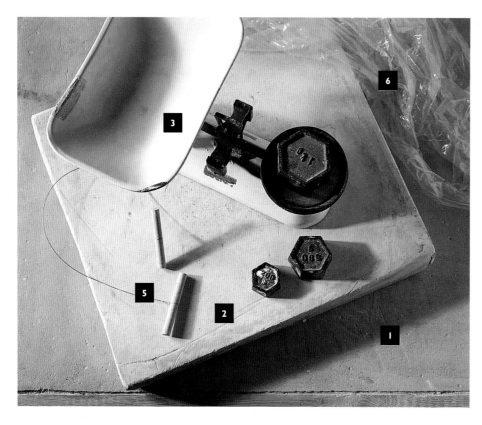

TECHNIQUES
PREPARING CLAY

Whether you use a handbuilding or wheel-based technique, you first need to ensure an even consistency throughout the clay's mass. This involves physically coaxing the clay into a homogenous state by wedging and kneading. A pugmill can be used for this process, dispensing with the need to wedge and knead the clay by hand, but many still prefer to wedge and knead after pugging to ensure that the clay particles are evenly aligned. A clay mass with an uneven consistency that has not been prepared well will be almost impossible to throw on the wheel.

Wedging clay

1 To prepare the clay for kneading, the clay is first wedged by cutting the mass into pieces with a cutting wire. The pieces are cut so that they can be rearranged to break up the distribution of the firmer and softer clay.

2 Lift one piece of clay at a time to shoulder height and slam it down onto the piece below. Reassemble and turn the faces into a new order to realign the firm and soft areas of clay within the mass. The new distribution of clay will now be easier to move during kneading.

Kneading clay

Do not attempt to prepare too much clay at one time. While it is valuable to have thinking time in which to finalize ideas and get ready for the "hands on" work, kneading is a rhythmical physical exercise and should not be made overly strenuous. There are two types of kneading: spiral kneading and oxhead kneading. The names relate to the shape that the clay forms. Both methods are equally successful – choose the one that suits you.

For either method, stand with your feet astride and with one foot slightly in front of the other and use your body weight to rock into the clay.

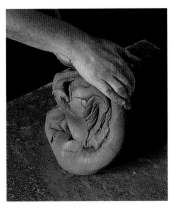

1A Spiral kneading: turn the clay with one hand and, keeping your arm straight, use the heel of your other hand to apply a downward pressure by rocking your body. Rock the clay backwards and forwards, turning the mass by a hand's width and repeat the downward pressure completing an entire rotation of the mass.

1B Oxhead kneading: fold the clay in on itself, using the heel of both hands to exert a downward pressure. Rock the clay up with your fingers towards your body and then down again with the heels of your hands away from your body.

2 Then cut the clay with a wire to check for lumps, air pockets and foreign bodies and if still uneven continue to knead, turning the clay by 45° before resuming.

This shows the spiral kneading technique with porcelain clay.

Kneading in additions

Coloured clays for use in the decoration of a work are prepared at the kneading stage by adding powdered stains and oxides. When making colour additions to clay at the kneading stage, you should decide what colour to use and at what strength you want to use it. Whether you are using colouring oxides or commercial stains, the colours should always be added to a light- or white-coloured base clay body to obtain a good colour response.

Before kneading in stains and oxides, calculate the dry weight of both your colour addition and the clay to achieve a controlled colour. As 30 per cent of wet clay is water, 150 g (5 oz) of wet clay is approximately equal to 100 g ($3\frac{3}{4}$ oz) dry weight. Once the dry weight of your clay is calculated weigh the stain or oxide to give the desired percentage of colour shading. Moisten the stain before starting the kneading to help distribute it evenly.

Cut through the clay and check that the additions are distributed evenly or unevenly as desired.

If you are using commercial stains for colouring clay, then remember that each stain will vary in its colour strength. Generally a darker colour will need a lower percentage of colour to give it a strong colour stain.

Experiment with colour additions of anything from 1–10 per cent. Note however that the blue oxides need only up to 2 per cent to give a strong blue.

To be more certain of the eventual colour of your work you might also choose to carry out a number of fired test pieces to see the colour strength of the fired clay for different percentages of added colour.

As well as colour additions, materials such as sand, grog or mica can be added to plastic clay to create clay which, when fired, will be ovenproof. These materials can also be kneaded into the clay to reduce the shrinkage rate (see clay shrinkage) or to add texture or colour.

Reclaiming clay

If clay has not been fired it can be reclaimed to be used again in its plastic state. To prepare clay for reconstitution you must first leave it to become bone dry – break or cut it into small pieces to allow maximum air contact.

1 Once the clay is bone dry, "slake" it by covering it with water in a large, plastic bowl. Leave it to soak overnight until it becomes a thick slop.

2 Any excess water that has not been absorbed should be removed the next day by carefully pouring it out or scooping it off.

Note: The length of time needed to reclaim clay will depend on how dry the plaster is, the room temperature and the consistency and amount of clay being reclaimed. You can cover the clay in plastic overnight to prevent it from drying out too much. When the clay has reached a manageable state, remove it from the plaster.

3 Spread the slop in a 5–15 cm (2–6 in) thick layer on to dry plaster bats. It can then be turned to bring more surface area in contact with the plaster, which then absorbs moisture from the clay.

4 If necessary, leave the clay slop on the plaster bats overnight to bring the clay consistency back to a firmness that is suitable for pugging or for wedging and kneading. Great care should be taken to ensure that pieces of plaster are not scraped or chipped off the plaster slab and therefore allowed to get into the clay, as this will contaminate it.

HEALTH AND SAFETY

Many of the materials used in ceramics, particularly those for glazing, are toxic and should be handled with great care. Wearing and using the right equipment will protect you from any hazardous substances. Take precautions, especially when preparing dry materials, to prevent the inhalation of dust particles.

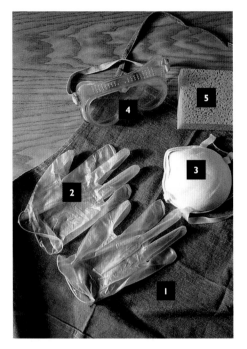

1 Apron.

2 Protective gloves.

3 Face mask that meets the appropriate particle size safety standards, BS6016 type 2 (dual cartridge respirator with a dust capturing prefilter).

4 Safety goggles.

5 Sponge for cleaning surfaces (avoiding dust creation).

Take particular care with the following materials:

HIGHLY TOXIC
- Antimony
- Barium

USE WITH EXTREME CARE
- Lithium oxide sources – spodumene, lepidolite
- Boron sources – borax, boric acid
- Silica sources – quartz, flint, frits, feldspars, clays
- All of the colouring oxides and stains and underglazes

USE WITH CARE
- Aluminium oxide sources – feldspar, clay, calcined alumina, alumina hydrate
- Sodium oxide sources – soda feldspar, pearl ash, nitre
- Calcium oxide sources – whiting, dolomite
- Magnesium oxide sources – magnetite, dolomite, talc
- Zinc
- Strontium

LEAD
Lead is a hazardous substance. Many makers use lead in their glazes, while others prefer to avoid it. Some low-fired lead glazes are hazardous and should not be used in combination with copper or chromium oxide. These combinations are not suitable for the internal areas of domestic ware. In addition, all glaze wash water from work with lead glaze must be contained, collected, recycled or treated as toxic waste. Only "fritted" leads should be used. A frit is a ceramic material that is fused with glass in a furnace and then crushed to make soluble raw materials insoluble for use in a glaze, and to make lead safer to use. If you are unsure of the composition of a particular lead glaze, you can take your work to a specialist laboratory for them to carry out a standard test for lead release on commercial ware. Lead should not be used when there are children around.

Ensure that you seek advice before using any lead in your ceramic work and protect yourself with a face mask (respirator) and gloves that meet appropriate safety standards.

When beginning to use glazes, use only commercially prepared lead-safe glazes and never add copper to them. Use lead only if you have a safe way of collecting all waste water and having it collected as toxic waste.

Safety tips

1 Never inhale or ingest powders.

2 Wear a safety mask (face respirator) and protective gloves when preparing glaze by mixing soluble materials. Wear gloves when using wet glaze. This prevents toxins being absorbed through the skin.

3 Wear a safety mask (face respirator) when spraying glaze and colour, or if incising, rubbing or manipulating dry glaze before firing. Use proper extraction equipment when using a spray gun or airbrush.

4 Avoid making dust at all times when preparing work or when cleaning up.

5 Keep working areas clean and free from glaze. Vacuum floors (wet or dry) or wash them down with water to a drain. Use an absolute filter that collects very fine clay and chemical particles if vacuuming a dry floor. Avoid sweeping, and any activity that will create dust.

6 Wear protective clothing and wash it regularly.

7 Store materials in carefully labelled, fireproof lidded containers and always check the instructions on raw materials carefully.

8 Do not store containers near kilns.

9 Keep all ceramic materials away from children and pets.

10 Never eat in your work area.

WORKSHOP LAYOUT

The type, volume and scale of work that you make will be the dominant factor in deciding the layout, size and location of your studio or workshop space. It is not always possible to site a workshop on a ground floor, but there are obvious advantages to this when bringing in heavy materials or moving out large pieces of work. When starting from scratch, it may be necessary to compromise on your ideal workshop by acquiring expensive equipment in stages, prioritising which pieces are most important and therefore those that should be purchased first.

The kiln

No matter how your work is made, there can be no finished ceramic work without the initial, and largest, financial outlay of a kiln (unless you use a communal one). It is possible to buy a second-hand electric kiln for considerably less than a new one, but check the model and number first and make sure you can still order replacement parts.

When purchasing a kiln for installation make sure there is adequate access through doorways, corridors or stairways to bring it to the intended site. All electric fired kilns, apart from the smallest, require an isolation switch and wiring in from the mains supply. Large electric kilns may require a three-phase electricity supply, which if not already present will add to the installation cost.

All kilns must be installed in a place that is ventilated near a window or extraction fan. Also consider whether its position will be practical for the type and quantity of work to be loaded into it. Fuel burning kilns require a flue or, unless located under an open-sided covering, a hood to collect fumes. Gas and oil kilns require a convenient source and access for fuel, as well as a safe storage place that is away from the direct heat of the kiln. Gas kilns can be adapted to portable gas where on-site delivery is not possible.

Floor

Be practical – flooring should be hard wearing and smooth to allow for repeated and effective washing down. The ideal floor for heavy-duty or large-volume production is one that slopes down towards a drain. A heavy-duty vacuum cleaner with an adequate filter and the capacity to take up water is a good alternative.

Water

Your main working space should ideally have a running water supply. Hot water can also make a difference when deciding whether to commence throwing on the wheel or not in the winter months. The sink should be large enough to wash out a bucket comfortably and its draining water should run into a settling or sediment tank (sink trap). This should be installed to take out heavy clay and glaze residue, preventing blockages to the drainage system and toxic materials entering the water system.

Heating and ventilation

In cool conditions clay can be uninvitingly cold to work, glazes will freeze in their buckets and cold fingers are unable to carry out any task. This means that heating becomes essential to include for the worker as well as the work itself. However, overly heated studios during firings, in hot summer months, or those in the Southern Hemisphere can create adverse conditions of their own. In these conditions it becomes a race against time to apply handles or slip, as the work will move from leatherhard to dry in the brief moments taken to go to the fridge for a cool drink. In hot climates, organize some sort of ventilation, create areas that avoid direct sunlight and plan an open-sided, working space to keep conditions as comfortable as possible.

Shelving

The type of shelving and storage you use will depend on the type of work you make. Makers of production ware will tend to choose an adjustable rack system. This means that long, narrow boards full of freshly made work can be easily transferred from the working area directly onto the drying rack. These boards or shelves can then be conveniently taken on and off the rack to turn the work for even drying. Large workshops in cold or wet climates will locate some form of heating near or under their drying racks to speed the drying process or prevent the wet work being frost damaged.

Storage, surfaces and power

As well as storage for ongoing work, you will need a space for the finished work, to store clay and glaze materials and large containers. Other large pieces of equipment, such as slab rollers, extruders, pugmills and blungers should also be taken into consideration when planning space or electrical installation with isolation switches. If you need a spray booth, it must be located next to an outside wall to allow for extraction.

You will require one or more sturdy tables or work benches in the main clay area and an additional area or wedging bench for preparing clay. And do not forget to plan your lighting – you may wish to place the main working table or wheel next to a window.

Organization

Plaster should always be kept separate from the main area used for working with clay to avoid contamination of the clay used for finished work. When trapped in the fired clay of a finished piece of work, plaster acts as a contaminant by absorbing and expanding. Any plaster that finds its way into a finished piece of work will irritatingly emerge from the fired clay or glazed surface months, sometimes years, later, leaving behind it an unwelcome scar. For this reason, ensure that all buckets and equipment used for plaster work are kept solely for plaster activities.

Planning

Whatever size of workshop you are planning, whether you make buttons or large sculptural pieces, take time to visit the studios and workshop spaces of other makers. Look at their layout solutions and ask about their kilns and equipment before you decide on a final plan.

You could also consider renting or sharing a well-equipped studio. Such workspaces can often be found in the classified section of specialist magazines or on noticeboards in specialist shops and organizations. It is sometimes possible to hire the use of a kiln and, for short-term projects or small quantities of work, this may be adequate. Some craft associations offer grants for setting up a workshop and purchasing equipment.

Studio layout

The photograph shows the working studio layout of a maker specializing in wheel-thrown work. The kiln and the sink with settling tank (sink trap) are sited on the other side of the studio.

1 Electric wheel.

2 Pugmill.

3 Scales.

4 Light for use when working at wheel.

5 Wooden bats for use on the wheel.

6 Banding wheel.

7 Paint stripper gun.

8 Heater.

9 Preparing clay area and worksurface.

10 General worksurface.

11 Storage area with adjustable shelving for finished work and work in progress.

12 Underbench storage area for clay and other large-scale materials, such as plaster or mixed glazes.

13 Work in progress wrapped in plastic.

14 Practical flooring.

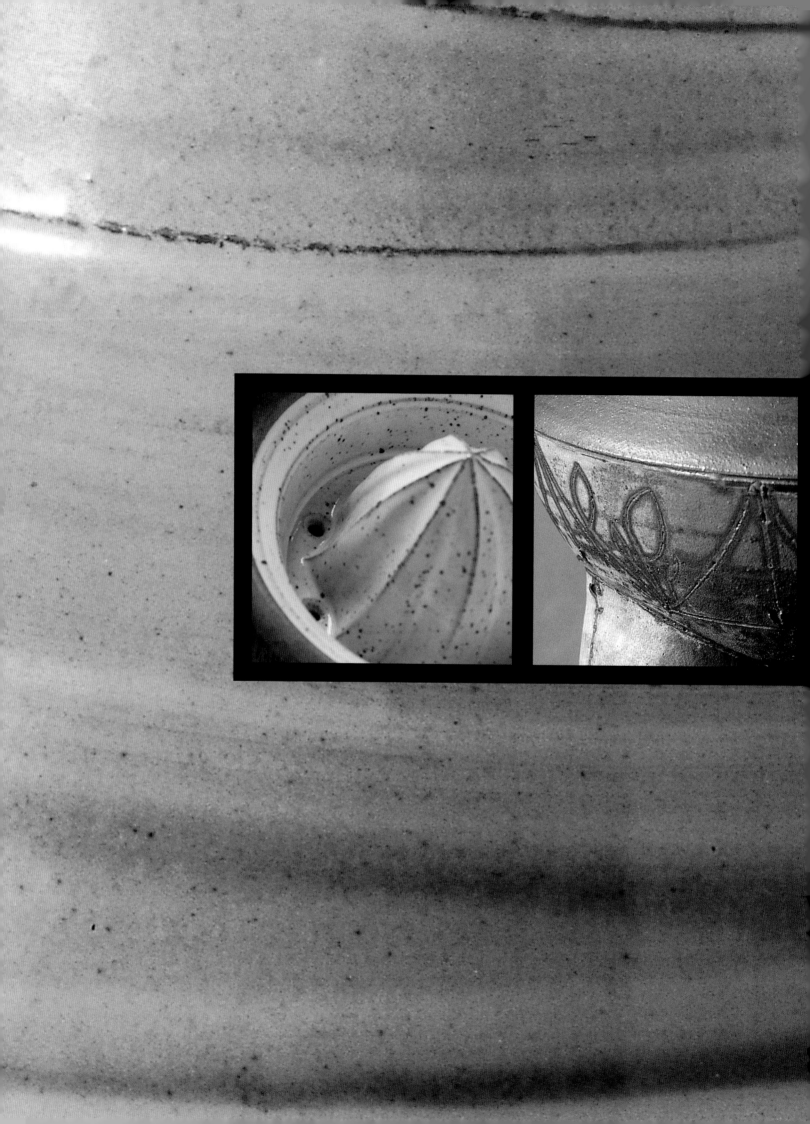

THROWING

ONCE, DURING A SUMMER HOLIDAY ON THE GREEK ISLAND OF NAXOS IN THE AEGEAN SEA, RICHARD PHETHEAN VISITED A SMALL MUSEUM THAT HAD A COLLECTION OF MINOAN POTTERY UNCEREMONIOUSLY DISPLAYED IN SEVERAL LARGE GLASS CABINETS. THERE BEFORE HIM STOOD ROW UPON ROW OF THE MOST EXQUISITE THROWN POTTERY VESSELS. BOTTLES, VASES, BOWLS AND CUPS WITH DELICATE RIMS AND HANDLES, BEAUTIFULLY PROPORTIONED FORMS, SIMPLE OXIDE DECORATION AND SANDY, UNGLAZED SURFACES. RICHARD PHETHEAN HAD BEEN POTTING FOR TEN YEARS. ALL THESE POTS HAD BEEN MADE OVER 4,000 YEARS AGO. IT HIT HOME INSTANTLY HOW WONDERFULLY TIMELESS THE CRAFT OF POTTERY WAS AND HOW INSPIRATIONAL SIMPLE, CLASSICAL SHAPES CAN BE.

EQUIPMENT
THROWING The earliest type of potter's wheel was simply a heavy, flat turntable – like a mill

wheel – which was pushed or kicked around by the potter (or a hapless potter's assistant!). This method

is still successfully employed in remote areas where only simple technology is required or available. Now

the electric wheel is widely used, but many potters still prefer the gentler pace of the kick wheel.

Kick wheel

Many throwers who use the kick wheel prefer its unhurried pace, which provides a more contemplative experience and results in less machine-like pots.

Modern kick wheels use much the same basic flywheel with a shaft mounted on free running bearings and a "wheelhead" on which the pots are thrown. Some kick wheels have a crank and treadle, and a relatively small flywheel. Momentum kick wheels have a heavy flywheel whose weight provides the power to keep the wheel turning. This is maintained with a kick directly onto the flywheel. The one pictured has a special notch on the wheelhead into which a stick is lodged to wind up the speed.

Electric wheel

An electric wheel is operated with a foot pedal to speed or slow the wheelhead. These use a variety of drive mechanisms and are controlled with a foot pedal. A smooth transition from slow to fast speed is important, and a steady slow speed is essential. Motor output can vary according to the weight of clay the potter is going to use and are usually between ¼ to 1 horsepower. The slip tray catches the water and slurry as you work, but should not be allowed to overflow otherwise the bearing housed beneath the wheelhead will rust. It is a good idea to place a shelf above the wheel on which to place boards or individual pieces of work as they are thrown. Keep water for throwing inside the wheel tray and ensure the throwing area is well lit.

Bats

Circular plywood or other composite material bats are used for throwing large or open ware. These are fixed onto the wheelhead in several ways:

1 A thrown clay pad or disc is made on which to stick the bat.
2 Bats may be drilled with two holes to correspond with pins screwed onto the wheelhead.
3 A "lotus" wheelhead is spoked and has a retaining lip into which a bat may be slotted.

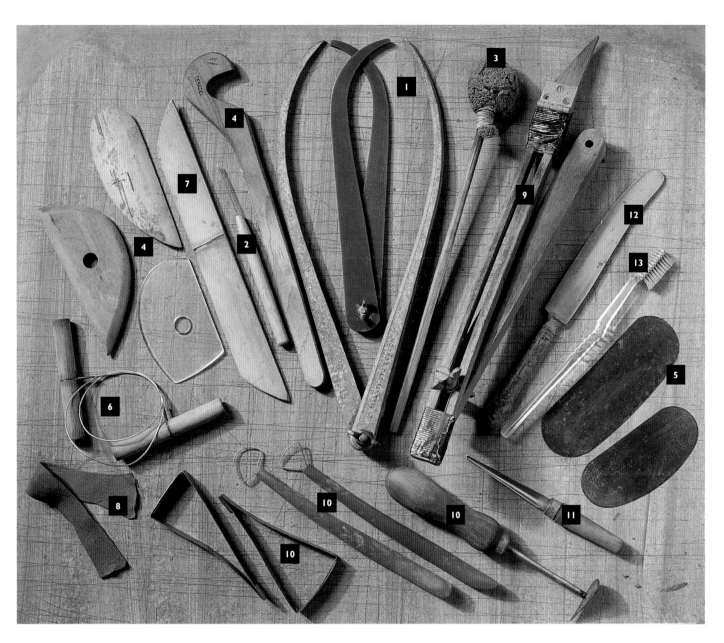

Throwing tools

1   Callipers for measuring widths of galleries (seats), lids and other fitted shapes.

2   A needle to cut top edges level while throwing and also to test the thickness of a base section.

3   A dottle or sponge on a stick to remove water from the inside base of a tall, narrowly enclosed shape.

4   Ribs for applying pressure while throwing, to smooth, compress and refine.

5   Metal kidneys to use in a similar way to a rib, but these pare away the surface rather than smooth it.

6   Wires (twisted and smooth) for cutting thrown shapes from the wheelhead.

7   An angled knife or bamboo tool for making a clean, angled base edge or bevel and making an angled notch to slide a cutting wire or twisted cotton into. These are also used for scribing lines on thrown shapes.

8   A chamois leather for compressing, smoothing and refining rims.

9   A pointer gauge for production throwing repeat shapes to a specific height and breadth.

10   Turning (trimming) tools for turning and paring the leatherhard shapes.

11   A hole cutter for cutting circular holes for teapot lids or straining holes.

12   A table knife for using like a metal kidney in tight corners.

13   A toothbrush is used for scoring and applying slurry.

14   A toggle and twisted cotton for cutting lids and small objects off a hump when throwing (not shown).

TECHNIQUES
BEFORE YOU START To begin with throwing can seem frustratingly bound in

impenetrable techniques, so an ordered preparation is vital. Approach the subject in logical steps, and with

patient practice your confidence will grow and tangible progress will be achieved.

No other pottery technique requires the clay to be quite as well prepared for successful progress as throwing (see preparing clay). Have a good supply of homogenous, de-aired, soft plastic clay balled up into 300–500 g (10 oz–1 lb) pieces stored in an airtight container, such as a lidded bucket. Also have a large sponge, a bowl of water, a basic tool kit, including a rib, needle, chamois, bevelling tool, dottle or sponge on a stick, cutting wire, and a hand towel within easy reach.

Wheel speed
Electric pottery wheels spin at up to 300 rpm. This top speed is only useful to experienced, fast production potters. In principle it is advisable to throw at much slower speeds, especially if you are a beginner, as the resulting pots will have more personality. The whole experience will also be less intimidating and frenetic, and much more contemplative and enjoyable. Throwing is a decelerating process from start to finish. Start at a top speed of between 100–150 rpm, a medium speed of between 50–100 rpm and a slow speed of between 10–50 rpm.

Body position
Do not be afraid of the clay. Sit closely into the slip tray and lean over the wheel-head in a dominant position. Always look for comfortable and effective methods to brace and control your hands and arms. Your hands should always be working together and preferably linked as if they are the hinged parts of one tool.

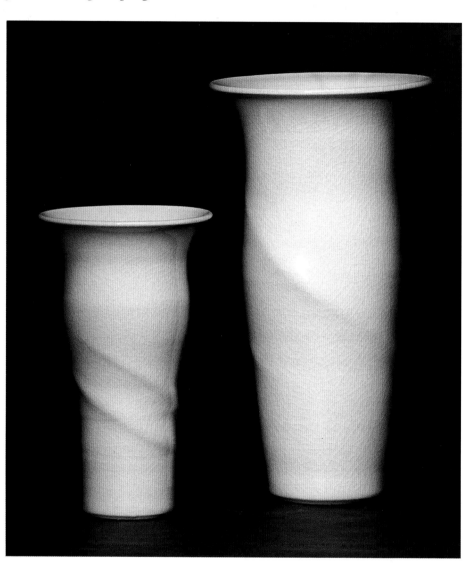

VASE FORMS (16 CM/6¼ IN AND 19 CM/7½ IN)
LIMOGES AND AUDRY BLACKMAN CLAY, POT RIMS ARE DRIED WITH A HOT AIR
GUN TO KEEP THEM SYMMETRICAL WHILE THE SOFT CLAY IS ALTERED, REDUCING
THE RISK OF COLLAPSE. THE MOVEMENT MARKS ARE MADE WITH A SMALL
ROUND STICK (JOHN DAWSON).

Water
This is your all-important lubricant throughout the throwing process. A container of water is therefore needed for all throwing work. Use too much and the clay will become saturated and weak. Use too little and the clay will stick, twist and tear. The right prescription is "little and often" – and should be sponged on, rather than poured. Ensure that you re-wet both your hands and the clay before each move and that there is always a film of lubrication between your hands or fingers and the clay surface. Lastly, ensure your finished pots are free from any pools and puddles of water before you remove them from the wheel.

The information in this chapter reflects an individual style and approach. Ask 10 different potters how to carry out a single technique and you will get 10 sometimes conflicting answers. This only proves that there are no hard and fast rules. You must simply regard all advice as personal. Try all methods and eventually you will develop a personal style of your own.

T E C H N I Q U E S
C R E A T I N G   A   S I M P L E   C Y L I N D E R The common, basic shape to a whole

family of pottery vessels, the cylinder is a simple form to practise. This exercise will give you the most

valuable lesson in the basic throwing techniques of hollowing, opening out and raising walls.

Centring (fast speed 100–150 rpm)

This action will form your rough ball into a smooth dome, which will spin without the slightest oscillation in the centre of the wheelhead. This is the foundation of successful throwing.

1 Ensure the wheelhead is clean and dry. Slap your ball of clay onto the centre so it sticks securely. Cup the first hand around the clay with your fingertips like a claw and rest your thumb on top, creating a "mould".

2 Bring your second hand to overlap the first and squeeze the clay into the 'mould'. Note how the arms are resting securely on the slip tray at 90° to each other. Now gently, but firmly, tug the clay towards you. As the wheel spins, the wobbling clay should begin to settle down. Always release your grip with a gentle relaxation, never with a jerk. Remember to re-lubricate with water regularly to prevent drying out.

3 This next action, which is called "coning-up", is a way of fine tuning the clay's preparation. One theory suggests that it orientates the clay particles into a spiral mode, thereby adding a little more evenness to the throwing process. Using the bottom edge of your palms and overlapping your fingers, squeeze and draw the clay up into a cone.

CUPS AND SAUCERS (8 CM/3¼ IN AND 10 CM/4 IN) STONEWARE CLAY, MATT WHITE AND CREAM GLAZES, REDUCTION FIRED (RUPERT SPIRA).

4 Keep your "mould" hand on the clay and move your second hand to press down onto it causing the clay to settle back into the desired flattened dome. Repeat moves 1 and 2 as necessary.

Hollowing (medium/fast speed 50–150 rpm)

At this stage the aim is to utilize all the available clay to create a vessel with walls and base of an even thickness. Walls that are even in any pottery making technique are perhaps the key to success.

5A In the orthodox method, a steady thumb is pressed down into the clay. It must be perfectly still otherwise the pot will become off-centre. Leave a base thickness of about 4–5 mm (⅛ in).

5B Alternatively, use your fingers to create the same result. Note how the other hand offers support and control in both methods.

6 An even base is created as the fingers open out the bottom of the form – this creates a 'doughnut' ring. The orthodox method would be to use the thumb as a logical progression of step 5A. Note how the fingers of the other hand provide counterpressure to maintain the width of the cylinder.

COPPER SPIRAL FLARED VESSEL (14 CM/5½ IN) THROWN PORCELAIN WITH A COPPER STAINED SPIRAL CREATING INTEGRAL LINES, EMULATING THE DECORATION OF PEBBLES (SUE PARASKEVA).

Pinching and lifting (slow/medium speed 10–100 rpm)

Essentially, the clay is pinched (pulled up) creating a narrow aperture through which the clay must pass as you draw your hand upwards, thereby reducing the thickness and increasing the height of the wall.

7 Now begin raising the wall. A simple and secure basic technique for beginners is a one-handed method with the thumb inside, the fingers outside and the other hand used for support. Each lift should be a steady glide from bottom to top. Lubricate before each lift. Here the fingertips are forming the pinch while the thumb makes a link. The potter's body should be forward with the forearms braced on the abdomen.

8 The "doughnut" is now converted into a good, evenly thick, slightly tapered cone. You may find it helpful to use the rib, as shown here. Push gently from inside against the rib in a rising action.

9 The wall is now taller and requires a more sturdy grip. Pinch your fingers into the knuckle and use your thumb to form the link (known as knuckling or pulling up). Lubricate and lean forward so your forearms can once again use your body for support. Lean backwards slowly to raise the grip in a nice, controlled lift.

10 Refine the finished cylinder with a rib. Use a chamois leather strip to smooth the rim by draping it over the rim and pinching lightly through the leather. A 325 g (11½ oz) ball should make a coffee mug-sized cylinder about 10 cm (4 in) high and 7 cm (2¾ in) wide when it is fired and finished.

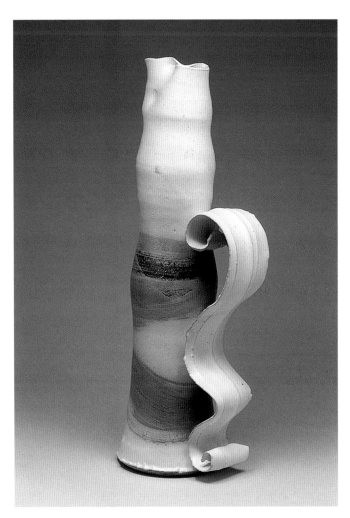

TALL JUG (58 CM/23 IN) ST THOMAS CLAY, THROWN AND ALTERED, TITANIUM CREAM GLAZE WITH BRUSHED OXIDE DECORATION. (KYRA CANE).

Cylinder sections

These pictures illustrate how the cylinder grows in cross-section, as the throwing process develops. This gives a clear visual demonstration of how potters adjust the form in clay as they are throwing. The subtle thickening is the secret to success in all thrown forms. It provides both wet and fired strength, helping to control distortion during the making processes and warping in the kiln.

1 You can check the basic thickness of the hollowed clay by pushing a needle through the clay to the wheelhead and resting your fingertip on the surface of the clay base. A thickness of 4–5 mm (⅙–¼in) is ideal.

2 The fingers open out a flat, even base creating the "doughnut". This puts all available clay in the right place for making the wall. Do not undercut too deeply.

3 The first lift creates a solid, even wall. See how the fingers are positioned to face each other through the clay.

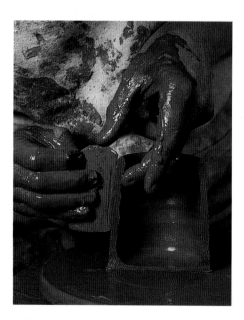

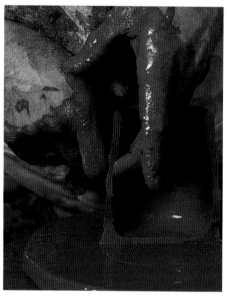

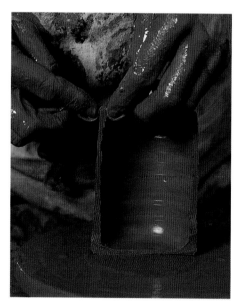

4 The rib consolidates and prepares the wall for further thinning.

5 Knuckling up (pulling up) to the final height thins the wall even further.

6 The chamois refines the rim. If you examine this cross-section closely, the wall is even, but notice how the rim carries a little extra weight.

Making cylinder refinements

These pictures show how a basic thrown form can be refined into a neat, finished vessel and then removed from the wheel.

Refining all your pots at this early stage is a good habit to get into. It preserves a lively freshness that can be progressively dulled

during subsequent leatherhard trimming and tidying. With practice, this method can be used to lift tall, cylindrical or bellied forms.

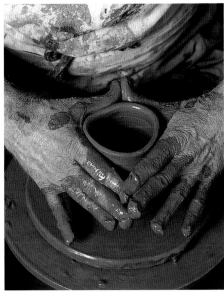

1 To maintain the correct development of a form, it is often necessary to decrease the diameter. "Collar in" by encircling the wall with your thumb and fingers, then slide the fingers across each in a scissors action.

2 Use a needle to trim an uneven or damaged rim by cutting through the slow turning pot towards a fingertip and lifting off the unwanted ring of clay.

3 Ensure that any water is sponged out before the pot is removed.

4 Make a neat angled undercut, or "bevel", at the bottom of the wall, otherwise you will be left with a jagged skirt. This bevel also aids accurate cutting off with a wire.

5 Hold a thin, taut cutting wire flat on the wheelhead or bat and pull or push it cleanly through underneath the pot.

6 Stop the wheel. Towel dry your hands and gently encircle the pot so the clay lightly sticks to your fingers and palms. Lift the pot off and gently place it down on a waiting board or bat.

Common cylinder-making problems

By cutting your pots in half you can learn a great deal, especially in diagnosing problems.

Each of these four cross sections shows the problems that can occur when developing a

cylinder form. Twisting may occur if the clay is insufficiently lubricated during throwing.

In this example the pot is short, thick and heavy because the clay is underused. The base hasn't been thinned or flattened enough, so the clay on the bottom cannot be used to heighten the wall.

This pot was off-centre when hollowing began, or was hollowed off-centre. As you start to raise the walls, the rim undulates markedly as the thick side grows more than the thin side.

This pot has been made fatally weak or has even been torn during the initial pinching and lifting (pulling up). The grip was too vigorous and/or the hands did not rise soon enough. Any thin or weak point within a wall will ultimately undermine your ability to further thin or stretch the form.

This cross-section shows the initial centred width of this pot. The wall has collapsed outwards forming a wider, shallower shape, but the corner is now so thin and weak that the base will probably crack or tear away from the wall.

BLACK OVAL BOWL (5 CM/2 IN) PORCELAIN, THROWN AND GENTLY BENT WHILE STILL SOFT. THE LEATHERHARD FORM IS ATTACHED TO A NEW HAND-ROLLED BASE AND SLOWLY DRIED (PRUE VENABLES). PHOTOGRAPH BY TERENCE BOGUE.

TECHNIQUES
CREATING BOWL SHAPES

The open shape of a bowl demands a switch of focus from the exterior silhouette to the interior's concave line. A second, distinct procedure called "turning" (trimming), carried out when the bowl is leatherhard, is used to trim away the surplus weight and create a footring (foot) on which the bowl form is cradled. Whether your shape is steep sided and enclosed like a cup, or shallow and open like a saucer, if it is curve-based, it is a member of this family.

1 The centred clay begins a little lower and wider than for a cylinder. Hollow it down to a clay depth of about 1 cm (⅓ in), then open out a curved base, gathering the clay into the familiar "doughnut" ring.

2 Pinch and lift the wall upwards and slightly outwards like the straight side of a "V", remembering to leave weight in the rim.

3 As the form grows, slow down the wheel speed. It should be slower than when you are working on a cylinder, because the rim of this wider shape is travelling faster and will therefore be more effected by the centrifugal force.

4 Now, in a stroke that begins in the centre of the form and rises up to the rim, the concave curve of the bowl is delicately pressed out, creating a smooth transition from base into wall. Hold your fingers either side of the clay, guiding the line of the shape, but no longer pinching. Use the rib to smooth and refine the form further if you wish.

5 The rim is refined on the finished form. Should you wish to make the form shallower, fold the rim gently out into a trumpet shape clasping your hands over the clay in a "praying" position, then regain the concave curve again using the method that has been described above.

Bowl sections

These pictures illustrate how the bowl develops in cross section. A bowl shape grows outward simultaneously, so a considerable thickness is left around the rim and immediately below it, as this will build up as the bowl swells outward.

1 Note that the curve and width of the bowl's base are already established, and how the doughnut ring is poised to be drawn up and outwards.

2 The initial bowl form is taking shape. Note the weight of clay at the rim.

3 The "V" shaped wall is further raised and thinned. The thorough throwing keeps the trimming and turning to a minimum.

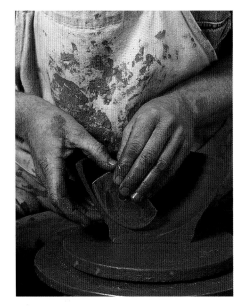

4 The rib is used to refine the all-important curve of the form's interior. Ensure that as the rib rises into the wall, the fingers outside the wall provide gentle counter pressure.

Common bowl-making problems

If the bowl wall becomes too thin and/ or too shallow the upper half of the wall can easily begin to slump. This is quickly exaggerated if the clay is a little off-centre to begin with or if the width of the clay is too narrow after centring.

A PAIR OF YELLOW AND A PAIR OF BROWN THROWN STONEWARE BOWLS (LUCIE RIE AND HANS COPER).

Repetition throwing

As your skills develop, you will find that your methods will settle into a pattern and rhythm. You can use this to establish your own style of work. Should you then wish to repeat shapes accurately, you must measure each one. When designing a piece of functional work for volume production, keep notes on the weight of clay used and its overall dimensions.

1 To make a run of pieces to the same size, weigh and shape the clay into balls ready to put onto the wheelhead. Beginners should take 12 or so pieces to the wheel to allow for uninterrupted practise. For a coffee mug, you need balls of 275–350 g (10–12 oz). Store them in plastic to prevent air drying the surface, and do not let them come into contact with a porous surface as this will also dry the outer surfaces of the clay.

2 Having weighed out your balls of clay, centre each piece to the same width using callipers.

3 When you are happy with the size and shape of the pot, use a point gauge to set the height and width without actually touching the pot. A gauge with a hinged tip is the most useful as you can swing the tip out of the way to remove the last pot and begin the next. Ultimately though, the character and personality of your pots will do more to give them a "family" resemblance than a pure measurement.

Turning a footring

Before turning a footring (trimming a foot), the bowl must be left to dry evenly to a leatherhard firmness. There are varying degrees of softness and stiffness within leatherhard, so it is useful to apply a simple test: is the bowl stiff enough to be stood on its rim and fixed to the wheelhead without it becoming distorted? And is the base soft enough to mark easily with a thumbnail, but too hard to make a thumbprint? If the answers are "yes" to both questions, then you are ready to proceed.

1 First, assess where to begin trimming the clay on the wall and the base. Above all, your aim should be to follow as accurately as possible the curve of the bowl's interior, creating an even balanced thickness and balanced weight.

2 Centre the upturned bowl, using the rings of the wheelhead to guide you. Revolve the wheel to check it is centred and then stop and correct if necessary. Fix the bowl using three coils of stiffish plastic clay on the wheelhead, evenly spaced around the bowl.

3 The width of a footring (foot) will vary according to the shape and width of the bowl, but will invariably be a third to a half of the rim's diameter. Use your aesthetic judgement and callipers to establish this measurement and mark the base accordingly.

Soup Tureen (38 cm/15 in) Thrown and decorated Earthenware (Fenella Mallalieu).

4 Use the turning (trimming) tool to trim the clay from the edge of the base. The first cut establishes the height and width of the footring (foot). Note how the blade of the tool is controlled with both hands. Rest your finger lightly on the spinning pot to prevent the bowl from dislodging suddenly. The pace of this technique should be "brisk".

5 The shape of the form is now trimmed out. A misjudgement of the bowl's shape at this point can lead to a bad weak point at a critical place where the wall meets the footring (foot).

6 The final trimming should be made inside the footring (foot).

7 Take care to examine the form as a whole. Regard the footring (foot) as extraneous and visualize the complete dome shape. This should correspond well to your memory of the bowl's interior. The footring (foot) itself needs to have a quality and weight to reflect the rim of the bowl.

8 You may need to remove the bowl and check progress once or twice during trimming. Mark one fixing coil and the bowl with a locating scratch, remove another coil and slide out the bowl. Reverse this and the bowl will return to its centred position. Finally, cradle the bowl in your hands to assess its weight and balance.

Trimming an upright form

1 Measure the base width and wall thickness. Assuming the pot's base is flat and even, trim the lower portion of the wall. Note the taller, fatter coils used to fix this pot in place on the wheelhead.

2 Trim the wall while keeping your other hand hovering over the pot to catch it should it dislodge.

3 The next stage is to add a neat bevel to the bottom edge.

Throwing on a bat

There are many occasions when it is preferable or even essential to use a bat. Bats can be made from a sheet material, such as plywood or chipboard. There are numerous systems to fix a bat to a wheel, but the method illustrated here requires no precision cutting or drilling – you simply stick the bat onto the wheelhead using a pad of plastic clay.

1 Centre about 300 g (11 oz) of clay for a 20–25 cm (8–10 in) bat. Use the side of your hand to flatten the clay into a shallow disc about 6–8 mm (¼ in) thick.

2 Use a rib to ensure it is perfectly flat, smooth and dry. Lie a ruler or straight stick across the pad to check it is not even the slightest bit thicker at the centre or the bat will not adhere properly.

3 Cut a groove into the surface and score a cross. This prevents the pad surface from becoming wet and slippery. It must remain tacky, but not wet.

4 Take a clean, dry bat and wipe the underside lightly with a damp sponge. Centre it into position and thump it in the middle to stick it down. Push it to test how well the bat is attached.

TECHNIQUES

CREATING FLAT FORMS

This is the last of the three basic forms in throwing. Here, base-making becomes the main and most critical part of the process. The clay you use can be considerably softer than that used for upright forms. It does not need to stand up in a thin wall, so a softer consistency helps with centring and flattening. A different, but equally demanding, set of skills and techniques have to be learned.

Making a plate

Use about 1.2 kg (2½ lb) of clay to make a 25–27 cm (10–10½ in) dinner plate.

1 Centring is the dominant part of the whole process. Note how as the top hand compresses and widens the clay, the fingertips of the hand underneath control its growth. The edge of the clay must not be allowed to fold over onto the bat like a wave, it must grow from below, pushing the water and slurry before it.

2 A wide, shallow disc is formed utilizing the width of the bat.

3 Make a hollow by hooking a thumb over the outside edge of the disc and drawing your fingertips across, creating a base thickness of 5–7 mm (¼ in). Use the fingers of your other hand to both support the move and compress the edge of the hollow as it grows to prevent the clay peeling away.

4 The desired width is achieved leaving the familiar doughnut ring at the circumference.

5 Here the base is put under compression as the thickness of the base is refined and subtly moves from the centre outwards or vice versa. This action compacts and binds the clay's particles, thus increasing crack resistance. The evenness of the base thickness is crucial as plates are particularly vulnerable to splitting or cracking as they shrink during drying and firing.

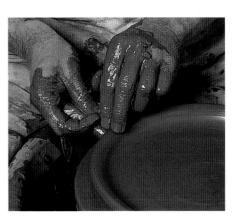

6 Use a rib to further refine the surface in a sweep from the centre to the rim. It is advisable to leave 1–2 mm (1/16 in) more thickness at the base's centre than at the rim.

7 Finally, pinch out and refine the rim into a suitable weight and width. When cutting off with a wire keep the cutting wire taut, level and on the surface of the bat.

TECHNIQUES
MAKING LIDDED FORMS

There are numerous ways to make a pot with a lid. Essentially there are two thrown elements, one of which has a retaining edge whereas the other is plain. Which method you choose depends on the function of the finished pot. This casserole dish form has a shelf or "gallery" (seat) on which the lid can sit.

1 Centre the clay and partially thin the wall before you form the gallery (seat). You will need a generous rim thickness.

2 Hold the rim gently just underneath, while using an index finger to cut a groove into it at a roughly 45° angle. Note how the thumb forms a link between the two hands.

3 Knuckle up (pull up) the wall of the pot to its finished height, taking care not to interfere with the gallery (seat).

4 Use the blade of a table knife to give the gallery (seat) a crisp refinement. Avoid making the gallery (seat) either too wide or too thin.

5 Stop the wheel to measure the gallery (seat) width with callipers. Do not be afraid to actually touch the clay surface to do this accurately.

6 The lid is a simple saucer shape. Centre and flatten as before, but not as wide as for a plate, and throw as if you are making a very shallow bowl. At the centre the thickness need only be about 6–7 mm (¼ in). Once again, actually touch the clay with the callipers to ensure you get an accurate measurement of the lid's diameter.

7 Trim the lid. When leatherhard, it becomes a gentle dome on which a knob or, as shown here, a strap handle, can be applied to create the finished form. The lugs are made from the same extrusion of clay used to make the handle (see handles).

A flange-lidded pot

Here the jar shape is plain, but note the weight and roundness of the rim.

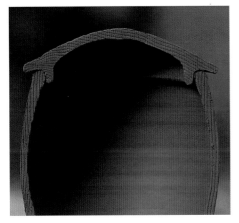

The lid is thrown exactly like a saucer, but with an upstanding flange. The aperture of the pot is measured to fit the outside edge of the flange. The slight overhang of the lid creates a good dust cover.

A cap-lidded pot

This "ginger jar" form is more enclosed so is suited to this cap lid, which needs a shoulder to sit on. Callipers are used to measure the outside edge of the raised lip on the jar as well as the outside edge of the cap to ensure a snug fit.

BISCUIT BARREL (20 CM/8 IN)
THROWN FORM WITH A
MIXTURE OF GRANITE, IRON,
ASH AND CLAY GLAZE
(MIKE DODD).

TECHNIQUES
HANDLES It is necessary to develop other skills than throwing in order to enhance the piece and extend the potential of wheel-thrown forms. Handles can be both a practical necessity on a pot and a way of giving further character, and they can be pulled or extruded.

Pulling handles

Of the many ways you can make coils or straps to shape into handles and lugs, pulled handles are the strongest and arguably the most akin to throwing. They are drawn from a stem of clay, giving them both the inherent strength and character of thrown pots.

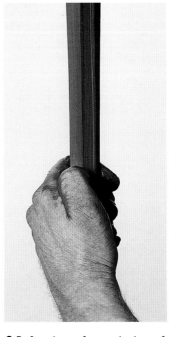

4 Lie the strap on a clean board, taking care not to kink, bend or otherwise spoil it. Cut it cleanly from the stem with a chopping action using your fingertips over the edge of the board.

3 Refine the surface and edges of the strap by drawing your thumb down against a crooked finger.

1 Several straps can be drawn or "pulled" from a tapered stem of well prepared clay. Wet your pulling hand and form a hole between your thumb and finger. Now draw downwards in swift strokes. Do not squeeze the clay, but rather let the friction do the stretching as you pull down.

2 Keep re-wetting your hand, otherwise the strap will tear prematurely. An elliptical section will give the strap strength down its centre and refined edges. Alter the size and shape of the hole in your hand to make handles suit the scale of the pot or pots you are working on.

CURL KNOB (DETAIL)
EXTRUDED, TEXTURED
AND MODELLED, SALT
GLAZED OVER COBALT
AND TITANIUM SLIPS
(JANE HAMLYN).

Extruding handles

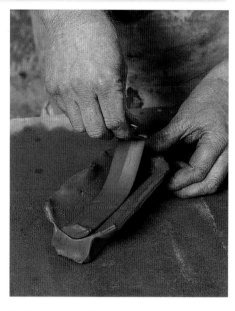

1 Extrusions are usually made by using a wad box (extruder) that forces clay through an aperture cut into a metal die. Here is a quick alternative. Make a wire loop with a suitable shape and size. Prepare an oblong block of good, soft carefully de-aired clay.

2 Hold the end of the loop in an upright position and draw it cleanly through the clay.

3 Do not allow the loop to exit from the rear of the clay block. Leave it in place while you carefully fold back the encasing flaps. Then lift out the strap using the loop.

4 Lie the straps on a clean, dry surface, ready for use. If you are not going to use them immediately, wrap them carefully in plastic – if they are too dry when you loop them onto the pot, they will crack or split.

LARGE DISH (33 CM/13 IN) HIGH SILICA BODY CLAY WITH ADDED FIRE-CLAY, THROWN AND ALTERED, MOUNTED ON FEET WITH A CENTRAL HANDLE ATTACHED, REDUCTION FIRED AND SALT GLAZED (MICHAEL CASSON).

T E C H N I Q U E S
A L T E R E D   F O R M S   Simple functional forms can possess great beauty and you may be happy

to focus on the technique of throwing bowls or cups. However, even the process of developing a jug or a

teapot that pours, involves an element of manipulation of the thrown form. The potential of altering

thrown forms is quite vast, and this approach often characterizes a particular style of thrown work.

In the projects chapter at the end of the book, you will be able to find a number of examples of how to approach functional forms in a range of throwing projects. The classic vessel forms created in these throwing projects illustrate how, with relatively simple manipulation, your basic throwing skills can be extended to produce pieces that have really quite a specialized function.

Inevitably, as your throwing skills improve, your standards rise, and your ambition to make ever larger or more complex forms also increases. While many contemporary makers enjoy the technique of throwing to endlessly explore the character and simplicity of familiar everyday pots, such as bowls, cups, jugs, containers and dishes, others seek to extend the boundaries of the vessel and of functional form by using the potter's wheel as a tool to create more organic and sculptural forms.

OPEN MANDALA (88 × 101 CM/34½ × 40 IN)
THROWN AND ALTERED, SINGLE FIRED IN LOW TEMPERATURE
SALT PROCESS. TERRA SIGILLATA SLIPS DEVELOPED FROM RED
AND WHITE CLAY (NEIL TETKOWSKI).

STONEWARE JAR (50 CM/20 IN)
THROWN AND ALTERED, WITH THICK, HIGH-SHRINKAGE
SLIPS TO CREATE SURFACE TEXTURE AND COLOUR, BARIUM
MATT GLAZED (ASHLEY HOWARD).

Arguably, the successful distortion and deconstruction of thrown forms is dependent on a thorough understanding and considerable mastery of the basic craft of producing the functional forms. This will make a difference both aesthetically and technically. Such experimentation can make your work more versatile and will lead you on to investigate other methods of forming clay, such as pinching or joining slabs.

Having mastered the basic techniques, your freshly thrown pots may then be pulled, stretched, faceted, pinched, squashed, torn and even dropped to distort their circular symmetry in a soft, organic way and enhance the surface with textural "distressing". Once stiffened, thrown shapes may also be cut and reassembled, carved and creased to build more angular "slab" or metal-like objects and vessels.

The most accomplished practitioners of this method manage to combine extraordinary and radical object making, while at the same time retaining the unique and quite unmistakable character and subtlety of the throwing method.

ABOVE: STONEWARE CYLINDER VASE (37 CM/14½ IN) STONEWARE CLAY WITH GROG AND FIBRE MESH, THROWN IN SECTIONS WITH THE WINGS COMBED, CARVED AND ATTACHED (COLIN PEARSON).

BELOW: BOWL OF DRY WATER (31 CM/12½ IN DIAMETER) THROWN AND ALTERED FORM WITH STONEWARE MIXED CLAYS, MULTIPLE SLIPS AND GLAZES (AKI MORIUCHI).

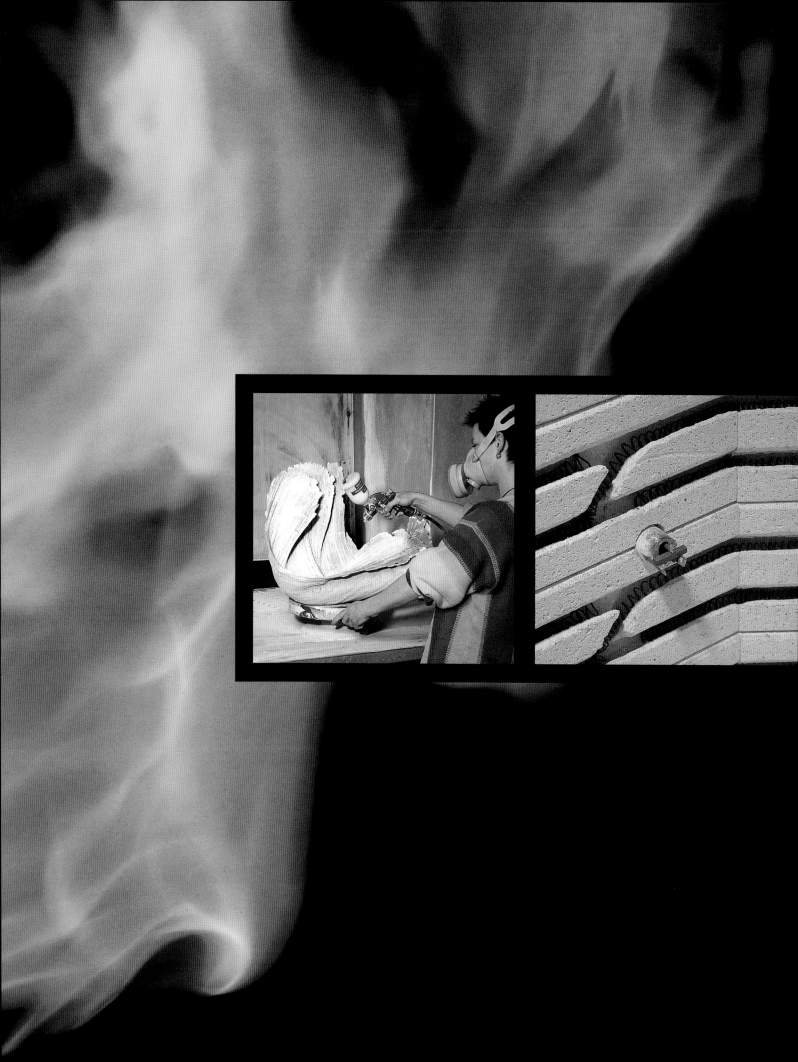

DECORATING, GLAZING AND FIRING

DECORATING, GLAZING AND FIRING ARE IN THEMSELVES DISTINCT AREAS WHEREIN THE SKILLED POTTER HAS A GREAT DEAL OF SCOPE FOR CREATIVITY AND ORIGINALITY. THEY ARE ALSO, HOWEVER, SKILLS OF WHICH A BASIC UNDERSTANDING IS VITAL IN ORDER FOR THE THROWER'S VISION TO TAKE SHAPE. WITH EACH NEW FIRING TECHNIQUE, EACH NEW COLOUR FOR DECORATING AND EACH NEW GLAZE RECIPE, KEEP A RECORD OF WHAT YOU DO AND OF THE FIRED RESULT TO HELP TO BUILD UP A REFERENCE OF SURFACE EFFECTS TO DRAW ON WHEN PLANNING NEW WORK.

EQUIPMENT
GLAZE AND DECORATION

Both the basic glazing and decoration equipment, such as brushes or buckets, and the more specialist equipment, such as sieves or masks (respirators), are available from ceramic suppliers. Spraying equipment involves a greater financial outlay, and is unnecessary if your preferred methods of applying glaze and colour are by brush, dipping or pouring.

Equipment for preparing ceramic colour and glaze

Even if buying your glaze as powders ready made, there is often a certain amount of weighing and preparation involved. All the equipment listed here is a standard range, which will be essential for this stage of work.

1   Accurate scales and weights for large (1a) and small (1b) quantities are used for weighing glaze ingredients, particularly colour additions or small quantities of test ingredients. When weighing out, check items off as you go in case of interruption.

2   Sieves are used for sieving ceramic colour. Mesh sizes vary, measured by holes per square inch. An optimum for ceramic colour is a 60–80 size mesh. Test sieves (2a) are used for smaller amounts and large sieves (2b) for larger quantities.

3   Sieve brush for pushing materials through a sieve.

4   Support slats for supporting sieves over a bucket.

5   Mortar and pestle for crushing stubborn materials before passing through a sieve and returning them to the mix.

6   Bucket and a range of plastic ware suitable for safe, airtight storage and for transferring materials.

7   Indelible pen for labelling buckets, as many mixed recipes look very similar once in slop form.

Equipment for applying glazes

8   A spray gun (8a) and compressor (8b) are used with a spray booth to apply colour or glaze when a flat, even application or a diffused quality is required. They are useful when you have only a small quantity of glaze. A spray gun is linked to a compressor via a flexible air hose. Airbrushes can also be used to spray small areas of decorative colour.

9   Glazing claw for gripping work when using a glaze that is susceptible to pouring and finger hold marks.

10   Safety mask or respirator (see health and safety) and gloves (not shown).

11   Brushes for applying glaze colour.

12   Measuring jug (cup) for pouring or transferring glaze.

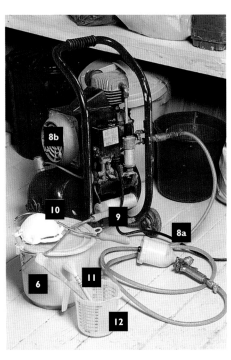

EQUIPMENT
FIRING EQUIPMENT
Brick-built kilns all work on the same principle of an enclosed construction in which the work to be fired is placed. Radiated or combusted heat flows freely around the ware and is directed in its circulation or draught either through, down or up, or as a combination, towards a flue. The heat climbs at a controlled rate until a desired temperature has been reached.

Kilns

The choice of whether to install a gas or electric kiln and whether it loads from the top or front is a personal preference combined with practical factors, for example which fuel is available and affordable, the size of kiln you require and where it is to be located.

All kilns require adequate ventilation as firing creates noxious and often toxic fumes, so if yours is to be located indoors, it is essential to have fume extraction via a fan and/or a chimney hood. Reduction firings with gas, oil or wood-fired kilns produce carbon monoxide so in this case ensure that the kiln is sited outside or away from the main working area.

There are many different styles of kilns so it is advisable to take a good look at what is available as well as assessing all the practical factors.

This front loading kiln might typically be used by a single maker regularly firing quantities of production ware. Alternatively the cost of this essential piece of equipment could also be shared between those working in the same space.

Lightweight refractory bricks retained in a stainless steel casing provide efficient insulation on top loading kilns, making them economical to fire. Top loaders are lighter and therefore easier to move and transport than front-loading kilns. Some gas-fired top loaders are built in interlocking sections enabling the firing chamber to be adjusted according to the size or quantity of work making them economical to fire.

Pyrometers

A pyrometer is an instrument that indicates the temperature of the firing chamber inside the kiln. It is housed outside the kiln and is linked to a thermocouple inside a porcelain sheath, which is fitted through the wall of the kiln and protrudes into the firing chamber. A thermocouple works by sensing heat with the help of two wires in different metals that are joined together at one end.

A small electric current is generated when the junction of the two wires is heated. The greater the amount of heat applied to the junction, the greater will be the voltage generated by the wires. There are several types of thermocouples and the amount of voltage generated at any particular temperature differs with each type. For this reason temperature indicators and controllers have to be calibrated for a particular thermocouple type and cannot be used with each other.

Controllers

This piece of equipment controls the firing temperature of the kiln. There are various controllers on the market ranging from those that just provide a cut-off point at the final firing temperature to those that enable control over the entire firing cycle. The required firing temperature is preset into the controller. Other points of the firing cycle can be preset with a controller, from the time firing begins (delay start) to the set points at which the rate of temperature is increased and also the rate of temperature increase (ramps). Other controller functions include the control of the latter or middle part of a firing called "soaking" where the kiln temperature is held at a fixed point for a measured amount of time. More complex controllers enable a number of firing programmes to be entered and stored ready for appropriate selection according to the type of firing required.

Many controllers also indicate the temperature of the firing chamber as the firing progresses, therefore also acting as a pyrometer.

Kiln sitters and limit timers

Many top loading electric kilns are fitted with kiln sitters, which turn the kiln off at the end of a firing cycle. A small orton cone or minibar inside the kiln (see photograph top right) dictates the point at which a weighted switching device cuts off the kiln's electricity supply. The kiln sitter does not allow automatic soaking at the end of a firing cycle, but it can be manually set for firing by lifting the counterweight and pressing the button to reset the kiln energy regulators to a lower setting. The kiln sitter is a reliable way of programming the end of the firing cycle, with the advantage of being triggered by active heat or heatwork (see glaze firing) and not by temperature alone.

The limit timer controls the temperature at which the kiln is turned off.

A kiln sitter (automatic cut off device) is set with the appropriate minibar cone, which melts at the end temperature and releases the cut off weight.

Gas burner and adjustment valve

Reduction in gas, oil or wood fired kilns is indicated by the length and type of flame you can see through the spy holes and flue. The burner's fuel intake and the secondary air supply are adjusted and the flue damper is partially closed to regulate the kiln's atmosphere until the correct reduction conditions occur. An oxidizing or neutral flame is blue, clear and straight, whereas a reduction flame is orange and curls and licks.

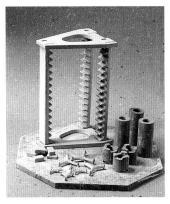

Stilts, shelves, piers and racks

Kiln furniture is made from a high firing refractory material that can withstand high temperatures without warping. It is used for separating work in the kiln, while making full and economic use of the space in the firing chamber. Kiln shelves are stacked alternately on three tiers of kiln props (kiln bricks) set directly above one another at each layer. Stilts are used to support work with glazed bases to prevent contact with the kiln shelves. Flat objects such as tiles and plates require a lot of shelf space and are uneconomic to fire without the use of racks. A selection of kiln furniture is shown above, including a kiln shelf (at base), a tile rack (back left), kiln props (bricks) (far right) and stilts (foreground, middle left).

Nichrome wire bead rack

The problem of how to fire glazed and Egyptian paste beads (which adhere to surfaces when fired) is removed with the use of a bead rack. Bead trees or racks fixed into clay supports can also be custom made with Nichrome wire, which you can buy from ceramic suppliers. Nichrome wire is the only wire that will withstand the high temperature of the kiln.

Pyrometric cones

Not all kilns come well equipped with temperature controllers, so it is important to have an accurate indication of active heat or heatwork, as opposed to the temperature registering inside the kiln during firing. Pyrometric cones serve this function. These cones are numbered according to the temperature at which they melt and bend. They are placed as far into the firing chamber as possible in line with the view through, but avoiding draughts from, the spyhole.

A number of different ranges of cones exist, including Orton, Seger and Harrison in varying temperatures and corresponding numbers, which do not run consecutively. The different ranges can be intermixed within a set of cones.

EQUIPMENT
RAKU EQUIPMENT

Raku firing requires the use of a kiln with an easy opening door enabling work to be lifted in and out of the firing chamber with tongs. A raku kiln is most commonly powered with combustible fuel and sited outdoors.

For pioneering potters, small raku kilns or large trolley loading kilns can be built to suit personal firing requirements. The designing and building of a kiln is a practical and viable solution requiring specialist high temperature materials and the necessary tools. Refractory bricks, ceramic fibre and aluminous cements and mortars are just a few of the materials necessary to withstand the high temperatures used in the firing process. Discussing your ideas with other potters before making final decisions about your approach is the best way to check out any pitfalls or adaptations needed to ensure the best design for your purpose.

1 Tongs used to place work into, and take work out of, a raku kiln.

2 Thick leather gloves to protect arms and hands from radiated heat from the kiln.

3 Goggles to protect eyes from rising ash when immersing work in sawdust.

4 Wire wool or scrubbing brush to reduce loose carbon deposits on reduced raku work (not shown).

5 Tin bath or metal container with sawdust for immersing and reducing hot work from the kiln.

6 Tin bath or metal container with water for rapid cooling and cleaning fired work (not shown).

7 Raku kiln (7a), gas burner and gas bottle (propane tank) (7b).

SOFTLY ENCRUSTED (54 CM/21 IN)
HANDBUILT WITH RAKU CLAY, A THIN
LAYER OF ENGOBE IS THEN PAINTED
ON. THE PIECE IS RAKU FIRED TO
APPROXIMATELY 1000°C (1832°F)
AND THEN COOLED IN SAWDUST
(KEITH ASHLEY).

TECHNIQUES
GLAZING
The sensitive application of glaze will enhance the colour, texture and design of a piece of work. However, the main practical reason for coating the entire surface of a domestic clay piece with glaze is to ensure that it is watertight, so that it can be cleaned easily and is safe to use for storing or presenting food or drink. The glazing technique you choose will depend on what you are glazing and how much glaze is available. The most suitable technique and the thickness of application is also dictated by the nature of the glaze you are using.

Glazing the inside of an enclosed shape

Enclosed internal surfaces should be glazed before any external glazing or colour decoration is undertaken. This prevents any unnecessary handling of applied external, unfired powdery materials or marring of carefully applied, unfired designs and glaze.

1 First stir the glaze thoroughly and check its consistency. Fill a jug (pitcher) and pour the glaze into the piece of work. Pour in enough glaze to fill the vessel as quickly as possible.

2 While turning the work in both hands, immediately pour out the excess back into the bucket making sure you have covered the entire surface of the inside wall. Any small spots you miss can be touched up using a soft brush or glaze mop and any excess spilled over onto the outside wall can be wiped back with a damp sponge.

The reason for performing this task with speed is to prevent the wall from becoming saturated. If this happens the glaze applied to the outer wall will not adhere. The wall will act like a wet sponge that cannot take up any more water, and the capillary action caused by the porosity of the bisqued wall will cease, therefore preventing the glaze particles forming an even covering to the surface of the work. If a piece does become over saturated either leave it until dry and then continue with the glazing or speed dry the work with a heat source, such as a paint stripper gun.

JUG (23 CM/9 IN)
PORCELAIN THROWN AND
MODELLED, WITH SLIP AND GLAZE
(EMMANUEL COOPER).

Glazing the outside of an enclosed shape

The work should be held in as few places as possible – at the foot or base to prevent unnecessary fingermarks of omitted glaze. Alternatively, and where possible, use a glazing claw (see glaze and decoration equipment) particularly if a piece is awkward to hold or the glaze is susceptible to marking because it does not "flatten out" in the firing.

1 Hold the work upside down and level to the surface of the glaze as it is submerged so a pocket of air is trapped inside, preventing a double build-up of glaze to the inside wall. Immerse it in the glaze quickly for no longer than three seconds to the point to which you want the glaze to reach.

You could also dip the piece base down, holding onto the dry inside wall. This enables you to use a different or contrasting glaze on the external wall, which will finish to a clean line at the rim edge. Plunge the piece in to the required depth of glaze for a maximum of 3 seconds being careful not to let glaze cascade over the top edge.

When removing the piece, tilt it to let any excess glaze drip back into the bucket giving it a slight shake to help any last drips fall away.

2 Slide the wet glazed piece onto the edge of a board or table rim being careful not to touch the wet glaze, and allow it to dry before it is handled again. If there are any missing spots, fill them in using a soft brush.

3 When the glaze is bone dry, you can pare away any touched-up finger marks or glaze drips with the edge of a metal kidney or rub them down with a dry finger tip bringing the powdered glaze to an even level. Pinholes in the powdery glaze surface can also be rubbed down with a dry finger once the glaze is thoroughly dry, but this is often unnecessary for fluid glazes will smooth out in the firing.

4 If required, a second overlapping layer of glaze (or selectively dipped areas) can be applied in the same way. This double dipping technique will affect the fired result and such overlapping glazes should be test fired first to ensure that one glaze does not cause the other to overly flux and run in the firing.

THROWN SKIRTED BOWL
(25.5 CM/10¼IN)
A CLAY MIXTURE OF RED
EARTHENWARE AND STONEWARE
WITH VERY COARSE GROG. GLAZES
ARE DIPPED AND SPRAYED AND THE
PIECE IS THEN OXIDATION FIRED
(RAY SILVERMAN).
PHOTOGRAPH BY HOWARD SHOOTER.

Dipping a tile or small object

Small objects are dipped using the same technique as glazing the outside of an enclosed shape. If glazing a number of small objects ensure the glaze is stirred frequently as glaze allowed to settle, even for a short time, will not give an adequate covering.

Eggcups, for example, can be dipped with a quick once up and down jerking action while under the glaze to dispel the trapped air pocket and pull glaze over the internal walls.

Pouring glaze for external walls

It is often easier to use a pouring technique for glazing ceramic pieces. This might be suitable if there is insufficient glaze to fully immerse a large piece of work, if spraying equipment is not available or if the glaze is inappropriate for brushing.

Invert the piece, resting it on level slats over a large container. Pour glaze down the side of the piece, covering as much of the surface as possible. Try not to overlap the glaze unless this is effect you desire. Small, missed areas can be spot patched rather than making the applied glaze overly thick.

Glazing external walls in this way tends to cause drops of dried glaze to accumulate at the rim and around any points that are resting on the slats, so it can be a laborious technique that requires careful scraping once the glaze is dry to level the surface. To avoid unnecessary handling, wipe the bases clean of glaze while the piece is still inverted. The powdered glaze will damage when dry, particularly at the top edge or rim if it is knocked.

Pouring is used for the Three-Footed Bowl throwing project because overlapping the glaze gives a multi-coloured effect where the thicknesses vary..

Glazing open shapes

1 Glaze the top face of a plate, saucer or any other flat shape first. If you do not have a glaze claw and there is not enough glaze to fully immerse the open shape, the glaze should first be poured on the front face, tilting the edges and using a swilling motion to cover the surface. The excess is poured out and splashes to the back face wiped back after the piece has been allowed to become dry to the touch.

2 To glaze the bottom face of an open shape, immerse it by holding the rim in two places and supporting the back with your thumbs.

If there is a foot rim you can hold, this is the better alternative, leaving fewer fingermarks to be retouched. Alternatively the back face can be poured one section at a time allowing the first to become dry to the touch before moving onto the next.

3 Alternatively, glaze claws are particularly useful for glazing flatware, such as plates and saucers, which cannot be easily held. Hold the piece with a glazing claw and sweep it with one motion through the glaze.

Spraying Glaze

Spraying is normally used to apply a "difficult" glaze that will not fire flat or that needs to be applied extremely thinly in a controlled manner. It is also often used when a soft, blurred, "disappearing" effect is required to edges of areas of coloured glaze. This is also a useful method of applying glaze when the work is too heavy or awkward to lift, or when there is insufficient glaze for individual, large pieces of work.

As with all glaze application, spraying should be done only when wearing an appropriate mask (respirator) and using extraction equipment (see glaze and decoration equipment and health and safety) as particles of airborne glaze materials should never be inhaled. Build up the glaze evenly, turning the piece of work on a banding wheel and holding the gun at an adequate distance to allow a wide spray that does not spot patch. After use, ensure that you wash spraying equipment with water to prevent the nozzle clogging up with glaze.

This photograph shows the spraying of a transparent glaze onto a textured interior. This spraying enables a thin, even application, which suits the nature of a transparent glaze very well. Pouring glaze on this piece would have resulted in pools of glaze collecting in the low points of the texture. Other "difficult" types of glaze that should be applied by spraying include those with a matt-fired finish.

Brushing a glaze

There are many brush-on glazes sold commercially in many colours, surfaces, fired effects and temperature ranges. They have a similar consistency to non-drip emulsion (latex) paint and are therefore easier to apply with a stiff brush. For a covering equivalent to poured or dipped glaze you will need to apply at least two coats, allowing the first to dry first.

These glazes are useful when using a small amount of glaze or if you require a particular colour or effect. Many slop glazes can be applied with a soft brush as an overall covering or as decoration. Glazes made up from dry materials should be tested for brushing as the technique can appear patchy and uneven.

Wax resist

Wax resist solution or hot candle wax melted with equal parts of paraffin oil (or kerosene) can be banded onto footrings (feet), bases and lid galleries to give a clean edge to the applied glaze and to make the important task of wiping back less laborious. 'Banding' involves centring a piece of work on a wheel and holding a loaded brush in a steady position while the work rotates. Ensure the wax resist solution is completely dry before applying the glaze so it will repel the glaze. Candle wax and oil is a highly inflammable mixture. If it catches fire, smother the flames with a fireproof material and remove the heat source immediately. Do not pour on water or use a fire extinguisher.

Cleaning back glaze

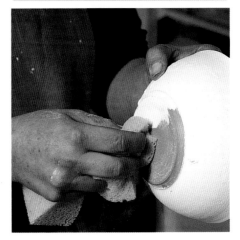

Any glaze must be cleared away from lid fittings where lids are to be fired in place to ensure a good fit. Bases, edges or points that will touch a kiln shelf should also be wiped clean with a damp sponge. This process is crucial to avoid the fired piece becoming stuck to a kiln shelf.

Spout strainer holes and lid air holes for teapots should be cleared of glaze before firing to prevent the fired gaze permanently filling holes that should be open. Do this, once the glaze is dry, with a needle or hole cutter.

Glaze can be left on a base if the piece to be fired is set on a stilt. Razor-sharp stilt scars can be removed using a carborundum stone (kiln brick bits) after firing.

MATERIALS

DECORATING
Decoration can be applied to plastic, leatherhard, dry, biscuit (bisque) fired, raw glaze or glaze fired clay depending on the effect you desire and the materials used. So that the decoration works as a whole with the ceramic piece and that it looks convincing, plan your approach to materials and how to apply them right from the beginning.

Colours for decorating ceramics come in many forms:

1 powders.

2 liquid form.

3 tubes.

4 pencils, felt pens and crayons.

5 pans.

Clay for decorating
The colour and texture of the clay you use will affect your decoration – a light clay will give a better colour response than a dark clay. If you wish, you can apply a covering of white or light slip to any of the darker clays, and this will respond to colour in a similar way to a light clay. Remember when applying clay as decoration (for example with modelling or inlay) it should be applied when the clay is still plastic or leatherhard. Clay can only be joined to dry clay when using fibre clay.

DECORATING SLIPS
Not to be confused with casting slip, which is liquid clay, decorating slip is applied to clay at the leatherhard stage. A base white slip can be stained or coloured to whatever colour you require.

ENGOBES
A mixture between slip and glaze, an engobe contains clay and a fluxing material, such as borax frit. Engobes can be applied in the same way as slips at the leatherhard or the biscuit (bisque) stage.

Colour for decorating
Oxides, underglaze colours and stains are available in many forms. They can be applied to leatherhard, dry, biscuit (bisque) fired clay and to raw glaze surfaces.

METALLIC OXIDES
Naturally occurring metallic oxides, such as cobalt, iron and rutile, are sold in powdered form and can be mixed together or used singly. They can be used to stain light-bodied clays and slips or glazes. Used as painted colour, powdered oxide should be mixed with water to the required strength, to approximately watercolour paint consistency. As metallic oxide particles are heavy, however, they settle quickly in water, which can cause application problems. To overcome this, they are often mixed with a little painting medium to keep them in suspension, or other mediums, such as china clay, glaze, oil or milk, making them easier to apply.

Metallic oxides have a softer quality than commercial stain colours. Each metallic oxide requires a specific strength of painted application which can only be learnt by initial trial and error and assessing the fired results.

Colour applied on top of a raw, unfired glaze surface while it is still powdery is known as "inglaze" because the applied colour sinks into the fired glaze, becoming soft and diffused as it melts in the heat of the kiln. This technique is also referred to as "maiolica" decoration when used in conjunction with a white glaze. Painted colour is often applied underneath a transparent glaze covering or a glaze with which the colour can interact.

UNDERGLAZE COLOURS AND STAINS
Commercially produced and sometimes intermixable, these are made up from a controlled blend of colour oxides. Suppliers refer to underglaze colours and stains respectively as UG and BS. They are available in a huge colour range in a number of forms and can be used for the same techniques as oxides. Underglazes, not in powdered form, contain carrying mediums, binders and fluxes. The colours are more stable and predictable than

naturally occurring oxides and are often used as a means of obtaining reds or yellows, which are difficult to achieve with oxides.

There is an often overwhelming array of underglaze and stain products available from ceramic suppliers, so always read their catalogues carefully to make sure that you get what you need. Check that colours, particularly reds and yellows, can achieve the right firing temperature for the clay you are using and the effect you require, as some will burn out at high temperatures.

- Powdered underglaze colours and stains are prepared in the same way as oxide powders either by mixing in water or with a specific medium. They can be used for staining slips, engobes and glazes.
- Liquid underglaze colours and stains are available in 56 ml (2 fl oz) to 568 ml (1 pt) jars. They can be thinned, but are thixotropic so they should be stirred before thinning. They are often intermixable and come in various guises such as one-strokes, which are transparent, or velvets, which are opaque and can be thinned for transparency or left unglazed for a velvet surface. Some can be applied to leatherhard clay, while others can be applied to both leatherhard and biscuit (bisque) fired clay. They can also be used to stain slips, engobes, glazes and clay, but powders are a more economical way of doing this.
- Paste underglaze colours and stains are available in 15 ml (¼ fl oz) tubes. Mix with water and a brush.
- Pan underglaze colours and stains should be mixed with water for painted application.
- Pencil, felt pen and crayon underglaze colours and stains are available in crayon, pencil and felt tip. They require pressure to apply, so they can be applied only at the biscuit (bisque) fired stage.

ONGLAZE
Also known as overglaze or enamel, onglaze colour is applied on top of a shiny, fired glaze and requires a separate firing. It is a strongly coloured, low-temperature glaze used for painting china. It is often laid on using various types of oils as a medium, but is also available in water-based formulations. They generally use lead as a flux and should therefore be handled carefully.

Commercial products
You can buy commercially prepared slips and glazes in powdered or liquid form from ceramic suppliers. The glazes can be selected from a catalogue in the same way as selecting paint from a colour chart. Ensure that the glaze is in keeping with the temperature range of the clay, with other glazes in the same piece and with other pieces in the same firing.

Base glazes
Commercial white or transparent glazes and white slips can be used as a base and varied by adding stains or oxides while in their dry state. Test the slips and glazes altered in this way before use. A small tile of clay is adequate for test samples fired to their maturing temperatures, but applying glaze to a vertical piece of clay will give a better indication of its fluidity.

To prevent spoiling a kiln shelf with unwelcome drips of molten glaze, fire test pieces on old or broken pieces of kiln shelf.

Single-fire decorating and glazing
Glaze is commonly applied to clay at the biscuit (bisque) stage of the clay cycle. Many potters, however, choose to single fire their work, applying all decoration and glazes up to and at the leatherhard or bone-dry stages. If the piece to be glazed is in two states, such as dry at the top and leatherhard at the bottom, cracking can occur between the two states so the work must be of an even consistency. Specific, single-fire glazes of a tested and suitable shrinkage rate should be used to fit these methods of working.

Single firing is a technique that has obvious time-saving, economic and ecological advantages, as well as allowing a spontaneous affinity to work that can be lost when work "reappears" in its biscuit (bisque) fired state. One potter who single-fires work refers to the break in continuity for the biscuit (bisque) firing as leaving makers "feeling alienated from the abrasive altered beasts that came back". (See Kilns and Firing for the effect the type of kiln and kiln firing has on a glaze.)

GEO-VECTOR
(35 x 54 x 36 CM/14 x 21¼ x 14 IN)
PORCELAIN WITH MOLOCHITE, SLAB MADE,
SURFACE COLOURED WITH SLIPS, OXIDIZED
FIRING (JENNY BEAVAN).

Using wax resist

Suitable for: glaze, slip, engobes and colour. Apply a wax resist to create a soft, broken edge dotted with random droplets of colour. The wax must be completely dry before any colour is applied in a milky to single (light) cream consistency. Lines scratched through the wax can be painted over with colour to give an etched line effect, which makes a good contrast to the mottled wax resist effect. Wax can be painted on leatherhard clay, biscuit (bisque) fired clay and on a raw glaze surface. Once applied, wax resist can only be removed by burning it out while firing.

Using latex resist

Suitable for: glaze, slip, engobes, colour and onglaze. Unlike wax, latex resist has the advantage of being removable to allow for further additions of colour or glaze to the blocked areas before firing. A latex resist must be completely dry before applying colour of any consistency. It leaves a sharper edge and cleaner finish than wax resist. It can be used to block out tight, graphic or fluid, painterly shapes. Remember to rinse brushes in warm water before the latex resist dries.

Feather combing

Suitable for: slip, but can also be tried with single fired glazes applied to leatherhard clay. The technique of feather combing is executed in two stages. The first is to trail a series of contrasting colour lines, which must sink into a wet, previously laid slip ground. Then use a bristle or feather tip to pull across the trailed lines on the wet ground. The slips should be a single (light) cream consistency and the decorating should be carried out as soon as the slip ground and trailed lines are laid.

Spraying

Suitable for: glaze, slip, engobes, colour and onglaze. A spray gun or air brush can be used to spray an overall covering of glaze or to create soft, blurred areas of colour (see glazing techniques). Spraying can be used in conjunction with stencils or with other resist methods.

The spray gun nozzle should be wide enough to suit the particle size of the medium being sprayed without blocking it. Remember to always wear a face mask (respirator) and avoid spraying work unless you have suitable extraction equipment or a spray booth (see glaze and decoration equipment). Colour and glazes are often toxic and inhalation and ingestion should be avoided at all times.

Combing

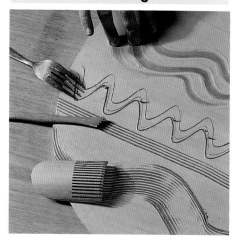

Suitable for: slip and glaze. Applied with fingers or any toothed tool on wet or dry mediums, combing creates lines, which can be straight or curved. Burrs of clay caused by combing into leatherhard or wet slips should be removed when the work is bone dry to prevent sharp fired edges of clay.

Banding

Suitable for: glaze, slip, engobes, colour and onglaze. Banded straight lines can be applied by centring a piece on a throwing wheel or heavy banding wheel and holding a loaded brush in a steady position while the work rotates.

SOFTLY-THROWN DISH (30 CM/12 IN) SLIP TRAILED AND BRUSHED WITH COPPER OXIDE AND PINK GLAZES (SANDY BROWN). PHOTOGRAPH BY JOHN ANDREW.

Marbling

Suitable for: slip but can also be tried with engobes, single-fired glazes applied to leatherhard clay and onglaze. Applied to leatherhard clay, marbling consists of laying trailed lines of fluid slip onto a contrasting ground of wet slip and tilting the work, traditionally an open form. As the wet slip begins to run down, the work is turned and tilted to allow the lines to run in a different direction. As the name indicates, the effect simulates the striations of marble.

Slip trailing

Suitable for: glaze, slip and engobes. Slip trailing and tube lining use the same method of drawing a fluid or raised piped line of slip. Slip trailed lines or dots are applied with a slip trailer at the leatherhard stage. The slip should have a double (heavy) cream to yogurt consistency and can be used in single or contrasting colours (the Throwing, Cup and Saucer and Teapot projects for use of slip trailing technique).

Slip trailing and tube lining

Tube lining is always raised and involves defining areas that are then filled with colour. It varies from slip trailing in that the tubed line can also be applied at the biscuit (bisque) fired stage when an engobe or glaze slip mixture is used. The areas defined by the raised lines are then coloured in or filled with oxides and underglazes which are further covered by a transparent glaze. Alternatively the glaze can be applied first and colours then applied to the defined areas.

TECHNIQUES
KILN FIRING

Once any forming and decorating work is complete the piece must next undergo the firing process to bring about ceramic change. The red heat and beyond within a kiln alters the nature of clay and glaze materials both chemically and physically causing them to become hard and permanent. Unless you are firing using an electric kiln with a control system, firing involves vigilance and attendance, often over a long period of time.

■ Many potters fire their work to an initial biscuit (bisque) firing of around 980–1100°C (1796–2012°F) to make the ware porous and give physical strength before decoration and glazing. The higher the temperature, the less porous the clay becomes. Some potters, who glaze fire to a low glaze temperature, such as raku or low earthenware, use an industrial technique of hard biscuit or bisque firing, when the initial firing has a higher temperature than that following glaze firing. This method provides a more vitrified clay body on low-fired glazed work, but can introduce the hurdle of applying glaze to work that is no longer porous. To overcome this, the high-fired bisque work can be heated in the kiln to enable a slop glaze to adhere to its surface.

Other potters omit the biscuit (bisque) firing process altogether and prefer to single fire. This shortens the long wait for the finished result and cuts out additional firing cost and handling time.

Temperature rise will vary widely depending on the type and size of your kiln, as well as the size of the work and the density of the kiln pack, so use the firing chart at the end of this section as a rough guide to firing times only.

SALTGLAZED JAR WITH A
CURL (35 CM/14 IN)
SINGLE FIRED, WITH COBALT AND
TITANIUM SLIPS (JANE HAMLYN).

Biscuit firing (or single firing)

Before any work can be fired it must first be allowed to become completely bone dry. Larger or thicker pieces of work must be left for longer to dry. The drying process is completed in the initial stages of the biscuit (bisque) firing known as "water smoking" – when, at 100–600°C (212–1112°F), chemically combined water evaporates and is driven out as steam. During this stage, vents in the kiln are left open to allow steam to exit.

It is critical to proceed slowly at this drying phase – too much haste will cause the steam to push open or explode the work. This creates a low, thudding sound in the kiln and is the death knell of probably all pieces of work in the kiln. Large or small pieces with thick wall sections – over 5 mm (¼ in) – are particularly susceptible to this, so take care. Leaving a biscuit (bisque) firing on a low temperature overnight with the kiln vents open is a good way to ensure work is safe to be heated further.

Once the initial firing has reached beyond 600°C (1112°F) or red heat, it is safe to turn up the heating rate, close any vents and proceed to the final temperature (see firing times and temperatures). The kiln is then allowed to cool and can be opened for unpacking when the temperature has reached around 100–150°C (212–302°F).

Glaze firing

As the kiln reaches certain temperatures (227°C/440°F and 557°C/1034°F) chemical changes take place that increase the size and formation of the quartz crystals in the clay. The first at 225°C (437°F) is known as the "cristobolite inversion" or "squeeze", the second at 573°C (1063°F) is known as the "quartz inversion". This quartz crystal change then repeats in reverse at the cooling stage. Particular care must be taken not to hurry the cooling of a glaze firing kiln at and around these temperatures by prematurely opening vents and doors. Doing so will result in fine cracks or dunting appearing. Sharp-edged cracks appear during the cooling process, whereas rounded or smooth edged cracks occur during the heating process.

Glaze firing

The final temperature for a glaze firing is predetermined by the glaze and clay body of the fired work. Glaze firing should be started slowly to drive out any moisture taken into the biscuit (bisque) ware from glazing. When the kiln is glowing at red heat or 600°C (1112°F), the rate of climb can be increased and vents should be closed.

When a glaze is subjected to heat, it interacts and fuses not only within itself, but also with materials on the clay surface it lies on. This is particularly the case in high-fired temperature or stoneware glazes. This reaction with the clay surface, called "interface", secures the glaze onto the clay. At low-fired, or earthenware, temperatures there is less interface of the glaze and clay.

The effect of heat on a glaze is subject to the amount of time a firing takes to achieve final temperature. This combination of time and heat is known as "heatwork" and it can only accurately be measured by pyrometric temperature cones or bars. Heat can also be gauged visually by colour, but shield your eyes with protective goggles and avoid staring into the glow of a high temperature kiln for long periods. At 1100°C (2012°F) the colour is orangey red, at 1200°C (2192°F) the orange brightens and at 1260°C (2300°F) it becomes bright yellow.

As the temperature rises, vitrification occurs when the clay and glaze or colours compact and fuse. As the final glaze temperature nears, glaze bubbles and craters form as gas escapes, which can cause the glaze defects of bloating or pinholing if it is not allowed to settle. By sustaining the kiln heat at a constant temperature, known as soaking, these defects can be eliminated. The kiln can then be turned off to cool.

Crystalline glaze firing

The rate at which the temperature is decreased determines the final size of crystals in a glaze. Crystalline glazes require a top maturing temperature of 1260–1280°C (2300–2336°F) followed by a rapid cool to 1100°C (2012°F) and then a prolonged soak to 1040°C (1904°F) to create seeds for the growth of crystals. Pieces of crystal glazed work are packed onto a foot or saucer to catch running glaze and glaze drips, which are ground off with a grindstone after firing.

Glaze temperature ranges

The temperature of a glaze firing varies according to the clay used in the piece. The ranges for earthenware, stoneware, porcelain and bone china are as follows:

- Earthenware 950–1150°C (1742–2102°F)
- Stoneware and porcelain 1200–1300°C (2192–2372°F)
- Bone china 1080–1100°C (1976–2012°F)

SLICED LOTUS FRUIT OF YOUR DREAMS, DETAIL OF CRYSTALLINE GLAZE (KATE MALONE).

SLICED LOTUS FRUIT OF YOUR DREAMS (38 CM/15 IN) COIL BUILT IN T-MATERIAL CLAY, CRYSTALLINE GLAZE FIRED (KATE MALONE). PHOTOGRAPH BY STEPHEN SPELLER.

Reduction firing

All kilns are capable of providing an oxidizing atmosphere around the ware during firing – this is where the circulation of air passing through the kiln is unrestricted. However, not all kilns are able to produce a second type of atmosphere, called "reduction", which involves restricting the passage of secondary air into the kiln and controlling pressure in the firing chamber with a flue damper. Reduction firing, used in conjunction with high temperature glazes or to produce lustreware, is achieved in kilns that supply heat through a burnt fuel, such as wood, oil, gas and solid fuels.

The picture shows a reduction flame at the spyhole of a gas-fired kiln. The strength of reduction is judged by the length and colour of the flame that protrudes when a bung is temporarily removed from a spyhole in the door, and the amount of smoke coming from the chimney.

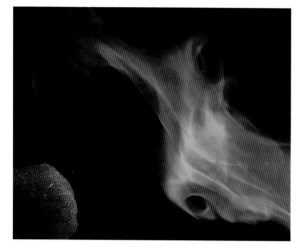

During reduction, the kiln's atmosphere seeks out oxygen to enable it to burn. Because the oxygen supply is restricted, the atmosphere grabs the chemically combined oxygen in some of the metal oxides contained in clay and glaze, producing an array of reduction effects, such as copper turning blood red, precious metals becoming lustrous and iron spot crystals being drawn from clay into the glaze surface.

Enamel firing

Onglazes fuse with the glaze on which they are applied at low temperatures. The temperatures can vary according to the colours used. This firing involves fusing colour into the softened glaze, often using successive firings to create overlapping mixed hues and depth of colour. Firings are relatively fast and require the opening of the kiln vent to allow fumes caused by the burning of painted mediums to leave the kiln as they burn away.

Enamel firing temperatures range from 700–900°C (1292–1652°F).

CONICAL TEAPOT CUP (13 CM/5 IN) CAST AND HANDBUILT IN SEMI-PORCELAIN CLAY. BISCUIT (BISQUE) FIRED, GLAZED IN A SEMI-MATT GLAZE AND PAINTED WITH ONGLAZE ENAMELS WITH SGRAFFITO DRAWING (MARGARET FORDE).

Raku firing

A traditional Japanese firing technique, raku is when glazed, biscuit-fired decorative ware is taken to its firing temperature very quickly. This produces a characteristic crazed quality to a glaze and lustrous effects to copper glazes. The hot work can be left uncovered to oxidize, quenched in water or quickly smothered in a combustible material, such as sawdust, to reduce the work. The clays used to produce work for raku firing are always open so they can withstand the thermal shock of the firing and cooling process (see Clay: The Fundamental Ingredient). Raku firing is an exciting technique with its spontaneous immediacy and its delicate blend of control and experiment.

The kilns used in raku firing can vary from an electric kiln (see raku equipment) to a brick-lined kiln. A downdraft kiln draws air down a separate stack on the side of the kiln, giving a more even temperature throughout the kiln and allowing the layering of work with shelves. An updraft kiln with shelves may tend to trap the heat, causing uneven temperatures throughout the kiln, although this can be overcome if there is a gap around the outer edge of the kiln shelf.

Raku firing temperatures range from 900–1000°C (1652–1832°F).

Raku kilns should be fired outdoors because a good deal of smoke will invariably be generated when unloading the fired items into the sawdust for reduction.

The glaze melt is used as a visual indication of when to remove the work from the kiln while it is still red hot.

Vapour firing

Salt, soda and wood firing are all types of vapour glazing. In order for salt glaze to develop, the clay body or applied slips must contain a certain proportion of silica, which is softened by the heat of the kiln and fuses with the sodium or salt. Salt firing is a toxic process producing hydrochloric acid fumes as a by-product so many makers who vapour glaze opt for the less polluting option of soda firing, which is less corrosive to the kiln and produces softer and brighter colours.

Salt and soda glazing produce effects ranging from the characteristic orange-peel texture covering the entire external area or partial flashing. The results depend on the design of the kiln, the kiln pack and the amount of vapour created. Pots and lid fittings are packed into the kiln on small wads made from a mixture of three parts alumina hydrate to one part china clay held together with a proportion of flour to make it into a kneadable dough.

TEA BOWLS (10 CM/4 IN) THROWN AND SODA FIRED (JEFF OESTREICH).

The allure of wood firing has as much to do with the physical process as the characteristic flashing and finished texture of the fire-glazed clay. The minerals in the ash deposits interact with the minerals in the clay, which fuse and form the glaze to the exposed surfaces of clay in the kiln firing. Wood is not only used as a kiln fuel for vapour glazing, it is often chosen as a fuel because it is readily available. The wood-firing process requires a constant vigil to maintain a steady temperature rise and to create the desired kiln atmosphere. For larger kilns this requires teams of wood stokers to maintain kilns, such as the "snake" or "climbing" kilns used in Japan.

Salt or soda is drip fed, sprayed or thrown into the flame of a kiln or through spyholes around the firing chamber at around 1240°C (2264°F).

Test rings, made of the same clay and coated with the same slips as the work you are firing are placed in the kiln in an accessible place. They are extracted to assess how much glaze has formed on the work and whether more vapour is required. Test rings are often placed in more than one area of a kiln because of temperature variations.

Sawdust and smoking

Pits or metal bins are packed with a combustible material, usually sawdust, around work for this low firing technique, which produces a characteristic patchy, black carbon effect. It is a technique often combined with burnished pieces and, although it seems to be low tech, it requires fine judgement on how best to pack the work and when to remove it. Work is often biscuit (bisque) fired before being placed for firing, which, if carefully controlled, can be successfully carried out on any clay body.

Glazed work can also be smoke fumed by exposing the fired piece to a reduction atmosphere inside a saggar packed with combustible material. A saggar is a lidded refractory box that protects fired work from direct contact with the kiln's atmosphere. This enables work to be reduced within an electric or oxidized environment with a greater control of the heating and cooling process. Ensure that the kiln and the immediate environment are well ventilated for this process.

WORK BY DUNCAN AYSCOUGH REDUCING AFTER A SAWDUST FIRING.

VASE (18 CM/7 IN) COILED, BURNISHED AND SMOKE FIRED (JANE PERRYMAN).

Firing times and temperatures

This chart gives examples of firing times for biscuit (bisque) and single firing, glaze firing, raku firing, crystalline firing and enamel firing. They relate to the number of hours the firings take to achieve certain temperatures and the specific temperature points at which the kiln atmosphere requires soaking or reducing. The term "soak" means holding a temperature in position.

Reduction for glaze firing temperatures can commence from 1000°C (1832°F) and continue until 1350°C (2462°F) for porcelain.
Italics refer to cooling temperatures.

HOURS	BISCUIT (BISQUE) AND SINGLE	GLAZE (REDUCTION & OXIDIZED)	RAKU	CRYSTALLINE	ENAMEL
1	50°C (122°F)	50°C (122°F)	300°C (572°F)	50°C (122°F)	50°C (122°F)
2	100°C (212°F)	100°C (212°F)	1000°C (1832°F) /reduction	100°C (212°F)	100°C (212°F)
3	150°C (302°F)	150°C (302°F)	100°C (212°F)	150°C (302°F)	150°C (302°F)
4	200°C (392°F)	250°C (482°F)		250°C (482°F)	250°C (482°F)
5	300°C (572°F)	400°C (752°F)		400°C (752°F)	400°C (752°F)
6	400°C (752°F)	700°C (1292°F)		700°C (1292°F)	700°C (1292°F)
7	600°C (1112°F)	1000°C+ (1832°F+) Reduction, soak at top earthware temp		1260–80°C (2300–36°F) (top temperature variable)	*600°C (1112°F)*
8	700°C (1292°F)	1280°C (2336°F) Reduction, soak at top stoneware temp		Rapid cool from top temperature to *1100°C (2012°F)*	*400°C (752°F)*
9	880°C (1616°F)	1350°C (2462°F) Reduction soak porcelain		*1040°C (1904°F) soak*	*300°C (572°F)*
10	1000°C (1832°F) Top temp biscuit	*1250°C (2280°F)*		*1040°C (1904°F)*	*200°C (392°F) soak*
11	*800°C (1472°F)*	*1000°C (1832°F)*		*1040°C (1904°F) soak*	*100°C (212°F)*
12	*600°C (1112°F)*	*700°C (1292°F)*		*1040°C (1904°F) soak*	
13	*400°C (752°F)*	*400°C (752°F)*		*Begin to cool*	
14	*300°C (572°F)*	*200°C (392°F)*		*900°C (1652°F)*	
15	*200°C (392°F)*	*100°C (212°F)*		*500°C (932°F)*	
16	*100°C (212°F)*			*300°C (572°F)*	
17				*150°C (302°F)*	

PROJECTS

THE FOLLOWING CHAPTER CONSISTS OF NINE PROJECTS THAT YOU CAN UNDERTAKE IN THE STUDIO. EACH ONE IS THE UNIQUE VISION OF THE ARTIST, AND THEREFORE REPRESENTS AN IDEAL OPPORTUNITY TO TRACE THE CREATIVE PROCESS FROM THE EARLIEST STAGES OF INSPIRATION AND DESIGN THROUGH TO THE FINAL EXECUTION. THE TECHNIQUES USED IN THE PROJECTS ARE SPECIFICALLY INTENDED TO COINCIDE WITH THOSE DESCRIBED IN THE PREVIOUS CHAPTERS.

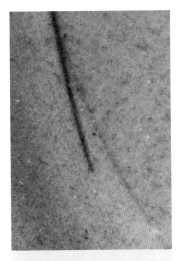

Cup and Saucer

The generous scale of this breakfast cup and saucer by Richard Phethean is perfect for the French morning habit of drinking café au lait from a bowl, or just for a refreshing cup of tea. Throwing both a flat saucer shape and an enclosed cup form will automatically extend your skills. A slip decoration technique is used, with wax resist applied to certain areas that will then avoid coverage by the slip and show the natural colour of the earthenware clay.

Materials
Spencroft sanded red
  earthenware 'green dot'

Equipment
Wheel and cutting wire
Rib
Callipers
Toothbrush
Turning (trimming) tool
Wax resist
Brushes for slip

Slips
White – white Devon ball clay
Light blue – add
  5% cobalt oxide
Dark blue – add
  20% cobalt oxide
Green – add 10% copper
  oxide and 1% chrome oxide
Thin lines – neat cobalt oxide

Glaze
CLEAR

Lead bisilicate	72%
Potash feldspar	13%
Ball clay	10%
Borax frit	5%
Bentonite	2%

HONEY
Powdered red earthenware
  clay is substituted for ball
  clay in above recipe.
Red iron oxide   ½%

Firing
Biscuit (bisque) fire to 1050°C
  (1922°F)
Glaze fire to 1125°C (2057°F),
  cones 03/02

1 The Cup This shape is very similar to the bowl illustrated earlier (see creating bowl shapes), but the base width is narrower and the footring (foot) depth taller. Take 450 g (1 lb) of clay and hollow and create a narrow curved base with a depth of about 1 cm (½ in).

2 Pinch and lift the wall into a steep-sided, V-shape, taking care to leave ample weight at the rim. If the rim is made too thin the handle's weight will pull the cup shape into an oval during drying and firing.

3 Refine the rim and subtly conceal the weight just below it.

4 Use the rib to refine and finish the curve of the cup's interior.

5 When leatherhard, measure and turn the cup's footring (foot) the same way as you would a bowl (see turning a footring). Then measure the exact width of the finished footring (foot) with callipers.

6 Make a pulled or extruded strap for the handle to a scale to suit the size and refinement of the cup (use a strip of paper and fold it against the cup to measure for length). Prepare the cup with a toothbrush where the handle will begin and end. Apply a blob of slurry to either end of the strap. Offer up and pinch the strap on the top end (good side facing the cup).

7 Place a finger above and behind the top join, loop the strap over and stick the other end lightly to the lower prepared area. Check that the handle is correctly aligned before joining (the cup can be stood on its rim allowing the strap to stiffen while it overhangs the surface).

8 The Saucer Centre and flatten the shape. Take 800 g (1¾ lb) of clay and hollow out the subtle curve of the saucer by leaving a clay depth in the centre of between 5–8 mm (¼–⅓ in). Draw the weight to the edge of the shape.

9 Pinch and pull out the full width of the saucer, taking care not to overthin the rim or flatten the shape too much.

10 When leatherhard, centre the saucer, right side up, and mark the well to take the cup's footring (foot).

11 Fix the saucer lightly in place and trim a very slight well into the surface.

12 Assess how much trimming the saucer requires and where the footring (foot) should come (its width should be approximately half that of the total saucer width). Allow the pieces to dry to leatherhard.

13 Mix the white slip base to a single (light) cream consistency. Half fill the tea cup with slip and empty it with a "tip and turn" action to coat the inside. Leave to stiffen, then dip the cup, held by the footring (foot), to coat the exterior. Wax the saucer around the rim's underside and coat on the top only, by tipping and turning. Once the white slip is dry, apply the coloured slips. Make long spiral strokes using a banding wheel. Biscuit (bisque) fire and glaze and fire.

Materials

Spencroft sanded red
earthenware "green dot"

Equipment

Wheel and cutting wire
Rib
Toothbrush
Serrated metal kidney
Wax resist
Brushes for slips

Slips

White – white Devon ball clay
Light blue – add 5% cobalt
oxide
Dark blue – add 20% cobalt
oxide
Watery green – add 10%
copper oxide and 1%
chrome oxide
Thin blue/black lines – neat
cobalt oxide

Glaze

CLEAR

Lead bisilicate	72%
Potash feldspar	13%
Ball clay	10%
Borax frit	5%
Bentonite	2%

HONEY

Powdered red earthenware
clay is substituted for ball clay

Red iron oxide	½%

Firing

Biscuit (bisque) fire to 1050°C
(1922°F)
Glaze fire to 1125°C (2057°F),
cones 03/02

Jug

This jug (pitcher) by Richard Phethean must be one of the most enduring and timeless forms since pottery was first made on the wheel. Once you become competent at making good, even cylinders, it is a natural and logical step to greatly increase the volume of the pot simply by stretching and swelling the wall. Today, large jugs are much more often used as vases, but as a form, with its handle pulled from the neck, it provides endless design possibilities.

1 Use 1.8 kg (4 lb) of clay to throw the basic form. In order to gain height rather than width, centre the clay into a narrow dome. Carry out hollowing, hand over hand, for increased force. Lean your body into the slip tray with your forearms braced against your abdomen for extra control.

2 Create a smooth, even base to the form before knuckling up (pulling up) the primary wall. It is important to gain significant height with each lift, taking care not to weaken or overthin the wall. Note the characteristic "chimney-pot" shape. The creation of this shape is crucial to your success at gaining maximum height. If need be, use the collaring technique to keep to the classical form.

3 Smooth and dry the pot's surface by pressing out towards a rib in an upward stroke between lifts. This is very helpful to reinforce the wall in preparation for further lifts.

4 Now that you can no longer link hands, assume a standing position and stoop over the wheel, with your arms braced against your body. This will provide the control and stability you require. For subsequent lifts, lubricate the wall, make a firm grip and lift initially by straightening up your body. Always ease off your grip towards the top of the form in order to allow the neck to retain its crucial strength.

7 Establish clearly where the neck of the form will begin. Collar in if required.

5 Create the belly by stretching rather than pinching. Use the minimum of lubrication and a gentle wheel speed. Stroke out the form with a very slow, rising push from the inside with fingertips against fingertips, or fingertips against a rib, moving up in parallel on the outside. The rib can also simultaneously smooth the surface of the pot if that is what you want. Tilt your head to watch the silhouette of the form develop.

6 Gently increase the volume with successive strokes from bottom to neck, allowing the form to distend naturally, as a balloon would inflate. Take care not to cause the belly to swell too much too low down, and not to create any odd corners or angles in the form's line, as this may cause it to collapse.

8 Refine the shape and character of the neck and rim.

9 Stop the wheel. Dry the thumb and forefinger of one hand and lightly place them against the rim to form the pouring lip aperture and width of the lip to suit the scale of the pot. Wet the index finger of your other hand and gently stroke out the lip with a waggling side-to-side action. Hold the finger vertically at first to create the throat, and then progressively more horizontally to create the "pout".

10 Prepare the jug rim to attach the handle, and a pre-made tapered stem of plastic clay, with a wet toothbrush. Then, stick the end of the stem firmly into place.

11 The form must be just stiff enough to hold its shape. Cradle the belly in one hand and refine the weight and length of the handle with the other and pull the handle from the rim. Add the combed detail with the serrated kidney. Place your hand lengthways behind the handle with your fingertips touching the neck, and the handle end resting on your wrist.

12 Carefully stand the pot upright, keeping the handle cradled in a now, horizontal position. Slide your hand backwards from beneath the handle and let it bend gently over two fingers of the other hand into a natural curve. Temporarily stick the lower end in place using its own surface slurry created during the pulling process. Adjust for length and alignment with the lip before welding more thoroughly.

13 Dip the leatherhard jug in white slip, rim first. Shake the drips off, then stand upright to dry. When the white slip base is leatherhard, wax resist the areas where slip is not wanted. Use Chinese horsehair brushes loaded liberally with the thin consistency slip. Make long spiral strokes by rotating the pots on a banding wheel. Biscuit (bisque) fire and glaze and fire.

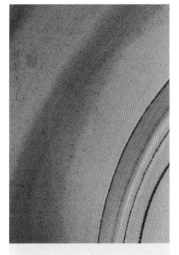

Wide-rimmed Dish

During the 17th century, when the Staffordshire potteries in England began to rise in importance, huge versions of this form, known as "chargers", were produced with bold, slip-decorated patterns and motifs. This presumably means they were used to carry food from the kitchens to load or "charge" the dining tables in the large homes of the wealthy. Richard Phethean considers them a great canvas on which to experiment with colour and pattern.

Materials

Spencroft sanded red
   earthenware "green dot"

Equipment

Wheel and cutting wire
Bat
Rib
Turning (trimming) tool
Wax resist
Brushes and banding wheel

Slips

White – white Devon ball clay
Light blue – add 5% cobalt
   oxide
Dark blue – add 20% cobalt
   oxide
Watery green – add 10%
   copper oxide and 1%
   chrome oxide
Thin blue/black lines – neat
   cobalt oxide

Glaze

CLEAR

Lead bisilicate	72%
Potash feldspar	13%
Ball clay	10%
Borax frit	5%
Bentonite	2%

HONEY
Powdered red earthenware
clay is substituted for ball clay

Red iron oxide	½%

Firing

Biscuit (bisque) fire to 1050°C
   (1922°F)
Glaze fire to 1125°C (2057°F),
   cones 03/02

1 This wide-rimmed dish will take 4–5 kg (9–11 lb) of clay. Place your clay lightly on the bat, turn the wheel and adjust the clay into a roughly centred position before patting the clay into a rough cone. With elbows out and hands facing in towards each other, gather the soft clay into a tallish cone.

2 Brace the forearm of your lateral centring hand on the slip tray or tuck it into your hip. Bear down on the clay with an upright forearm and let the fingers overlap and reinforce the centring hand. Do not allow the clay to "mushroom" over at the edge as this may cause air and/or slurry to become trapped in the clay.

3 Continue this process downwards and outwards, creating a shallow disc which utilizes the full width of the bat.

4 Hollow the centred disc to a base thickness of between 8–10mm (⅓–½ in). Claw out the base width using the fingers of one hand with the thumb hooked over the outside edge of the clay. Reinforce this move with the other hand and simultaneously compress the edge of the hollow to prevent it peeling away excessively.

5 Compress and refine the subtle curve of the base (this is vital to avoid cracking during drying). The pressure of both hands can move the weight either from the centre to the rim or vice versa.

6 Turn the wheel very gently, throw the wall upwards and outwards, but do not overthin it as it has to support itself during the final stage. Refine the weight and quality of the rim. Use the rib to dry, compress, smooth and refine the base and create the step before the rim.

7 Slow the wheel to a crawl. Gently lean on the rim with some fingers protecting it from falling out too far. (You may wish to leave the clay to stiffen before you do this.) It is a mistake to make the rim too horizontal, as this may cause it to collapse or droop in the kiln. Make a deep, crisp bevel onto the bat. Cutting off the bat with a very taut wire is essential. Leave the dish to become the stiff side of leatherhard.

8 Assess where the footrings (feet) have to come and how much weight can be trimmed away. Overturn your leatherhard dish onto a bat wide enough to take the rim. (Here the bats are used to raise the wider one above the height of the slip tray, or if you can, remove the slip tray first.) Rest the centre of the dish on a flattened lump of stiff clay during turning (trimming).

9 Now you should establish both the width and the depth of the outer footring (foot), and then centre up and fix the dish with three coils of clay.

10 Trim between the rim and the outer footring (foot).

11 Establish the width of the inner footring (foot) and trim away to the outer footring. Use the corner of the tool to create a spiral of concentric furrows as this causes less pressure on the base. Shave off the furrows.

12 Shave the very centre of the dish. Take care not to overthin the base at any point as flat forms are prone to cracking during drying or firing. Create the combed detail with a serrated metal kidney on the freshly-thrown clay.

13 At leatherhard stage wax the rim's underside and coat with white base slip on the top side, using the tip and turn method. When the white slip is dry, apply the coloured slips, with brushes and a banding wheel. Biscuit (bisque) fire and then glaze and fire.

Oval Baking Bowl

This oval bowl, designed by Nick Membery, is an example of a combined form using the techniques of throwing and handbuilding. The main form is initially thrown on a potter's wheel, then altered into an oval shape and finally joined onto a slab-rolled base.

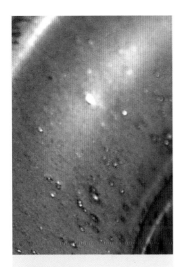

Materials
Stoneware clay

Equipment
Wheel and cutting wire
Circular throwing bat
Straight-sided throwing rib
Strip of thin plastic
6 cm (2½ in) oval nail with
    rounded end
Sponge
Rolling pin
2 rolling guides 5 mm (¼ in)
    thick
Rolling cloth
Patterned plaster slab
Banding wheel
Knife
Needle
Plastic comb
Toothbrush
Round-ended wooden dowel
Profile beading tool
Water sprayer
Gas kiln
Gloves for glazing

Glaze
BLUE GLAZE

Potash feldspar	50%
China clay	30%
Whiting	10%
Talc	10%
Cobalt oxide	0.75%

Firing
Biscuit (bisque) fire to 990°C
    (1814°F)
Reduction fire to 1280°C
    (2336°F)

1 Centre 1.2 kg (2½lb) of wedged clay onto a throwing bat and open the clay straight through to the bat leaving no base. Continue opening the clay to a diameter of about 14 cm (5½ in). Do this fairly slowly and push the clay firmly onto the bat throughout, otherwise there is a tendency for the clay to work loose when making pots without a base.

2 Cone the opened clay upwards and inwards with your thumb and forefinger, preparing to pull the wall up to the required size. Leave the clay slightly thicker where it joins the bat while you are pulling it upwards. This will help when joining the wall to the base later on. Once you have pulled up the wall start to fold over the rim from the inside using your right hand outside for support.

4 Finalize the rim shape. The rim is smoothed and compressed by holding a flat piece of plastic across it as it turns on the wheel. Use a steel nail to emphasize the start of the rim and the change of direction in the pot wall, both inside and out. The thrown wall of the pot should measure 10 cm (4 in) high by 25 cm (10 in) wide. Remove any water from inside the pot with a sponge. Lift the bat with the pot from the wheelhead, put to one side and leave to stiffen.

3 Refine the shape of the pot with a straight-sided throwing rib by pushing from the inside outwards onto the rib. This will also remove any excess slurry and the drawing rings (rims) from the outside of the pot.

5 Roll out a clay slab onto a cloth using guide sticks for the thickness. This slab should be oval and big enough for the base of the thrown pot. Dry it out for a couple of hours. When it has stiffened slightly, place it face down on a patterned plaster slab. Place the rolling cloth over the clay slab and roll it once more to impress the pattern into the base. Remove the clay slab from the plaster slab and leave to dry until leatherhard.

6 Place the bat with the thrown wall of the pot onto a banding wheel. Take a thin knife and cut the clay from the bat all the way around and then use both hands to gently push the bowl into an oval shape. The pot should be altered before it is leatherhard, but when it has dried enough to be handled easily.

7 When both the thrown wall and the base are leatherhard they are ready to be joined. Put the base onto the circular bat and then both onto the banding wheel. Position the oval pot wall on the base. Check the oval shape is symmetrical and mark the outline of the wall onto the base both inside and outside with a potter's needle. Remove the wall. Leave about 1 cm (½ in) extra all the way round the outside of the larger of the two marked oval shapes and cut away the excess clay from the slab with a knife.

8 Take a piece of plastic comb about 2.5 cm (1 in) long and score the bottom edge of the thrown wall and the section of the base to which it will be joined. Slurry the scored wall of the pot and press the wall firmly into position on the base. Wriggle the bottom of the wall slightly all the way round to ensure that it is tightly stuck onto the base.

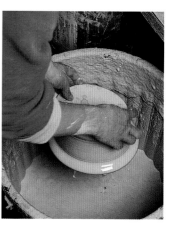

9 Support the inside of the pot wall with your left hand and move around pressing the excess clay from the base up and onto the outside of the pot. Turn the banding wheel and smooth the clay with two fingers, softening it with water if necessary.

10 Run a round-ended piece of wooden dowel all the way Around the inside of the pot where the wall joins the base This will help to seal and compress the join and will also add an attractive finishing mark to the inside.

11 Finish the outside base of the pot with a profile beading tool made from thin plastic or metal. Run the tool smoothly around by holding it in a fixed position and turning the banding wheel. This will remove the excess clay and finalize the beading at the base of the pot. Spray water around the bottom of the pot, as it turns to lubricate the beading tool.

12 Leave the finished pot to dry before biscuit (bisque) firing it to 990°C (1814°F). Then, wearing gloves, dip it into the glaze and reduction fire it to 1280°C (1236°F) in a gas kiln.

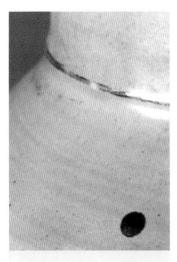

Sectional Vase

Richard Phethean advises that the degree of difficulty in throwing this shape in one piece easily outweighs the technical skill required to make and join two sections. This is because the tall neck of a single form would cause the belly to distort or collapse. The two smaller thrown sections are easier to make accurately and evenly, and the resulting pot will be lighter and more elegant. This working method will also increase the scale and diversity of your work.

Materials

Spencroft sanded red
   earthenware "green dot"

Equipment

Wheel and cutting wire
Bats
Callipers
Rib
Sponge
Needle
Table knife or metal kidney
Serrated metal kidney
Wax resist
Brushes for slips
Electric kiln

Slips

White – white Devon ball clay
Light blue – add 5% cobalt
   oxide
Dark blue – add 20% cobalt
   oxide
Green – add 10% copper
   oxide and 1% chrome oxide
Thin blue/black lines – neat
   cobalt oxide
Make up the coloured slips to
   a thin, watery consistency

Glaze

CLEAR

Lead bisilicate	72%
Potash feldspar	13%
Ball clay	10%
Borax frit	5%
Bentonite	2%

HONEY

Powdered red earthenware
   clay is substituted for ball
   clay in above recipe

Red iron oxide   ½%

Firing

Biscuit (bisque) fire to 1050°C
   (1922°F)
Glaze fire to 1125°C
   (2057°F), cones 03/02

1 Make a clear, visual plan of the form so that each section may be accurately thrown. The bottom section has a flat base and is thrown and bellied in a very similar way to the Jug (pitcher) project. It will use 1.25 kg (2¾ lb) clay. Good centring is vital for this technique to work well. Here, the rim of the section is being squared off at an appropriate angle.

2 Carefully measure the inside edge of the neck with callipers. Do not wire off the pot from the bat. Leave it to stiffen.

3 The top section, which uses 800 g (1¾ lb) clay, is made "upside down". The width at the base of the centred clay will determine the width at the top of the finished form. Hollow the clay right down to the bat and open out in the usual way.

4 Raise the primary wall into a narrow cone.

5 Achieve the final height and rough form.

6 Refine the concave top section with a rib. Measure and square the rim with callipers in a corresponding way to that of the bottom section.

7 When it has stiffened sufficiently, recentre the bottom section onto the wheel with its bat restuck lightly onto a clay pad. Wet the rim with a sponge and score thoroughly in preparation for joining. Similarly prepare the top section's rim and then apply a coating of slurry.

8 Invert the top section and bring it down onto the bottom section, aligning the joins carefully. Now slowly revolve the wheel to check if the top section is on centre. If not, quickly lift it off and realign before it sticks too well.

9 Turn the wheel and seal the join between the two sections with a table knife or kidney.

10 Release the bat from the top section of the pot with a cutting wire, using your breastbone as counter pressure.

11 Trim the top section with a needle and preserve it in a state just soft enough to wet and rethrow.

12 Rethrow the new rim and refine as required.

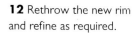

13 Once leatherhard, wax resist the areas where slip is not wanted. Dip the vase rim first in white slip to a single (light) cream consistency. Once it is dry and leatherhard, brush the coloured slips onto the white slip base. Biscuit (bisque) fire and then glaze and fire.

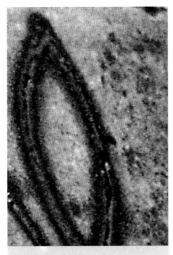

Three-footed Bowl

This pot was inspired by a collection of 14–16th century bronze tripod pots made by slaves of the Shang culture in China. Unearthed in 1955 at Chengchow, Honan Province, the pots were often decorated with animal masks and dragons and mainly used for cooking. This pot is constructed with four thrown forms and the maker, Chris Bramble, is intrigued by the visual dynamic of the three individually thrown pointed legs.

Materials

Iron-based stoneware clay
Manganese dioxide

Equipment

Wheel and cutting wire
Metal kidney
Plastic credit or phone card
Toothbrush
Sponge
Metal tool
Paintbrush
Needle
Gloves for glazing
Glaze rack and basin
Banding wheel
Gas kiln

Glaze

Manganese dioxide
DRY BLUE GLAZE

Feldspar	13%
Whiting	27%
China clay	53%
Soda ash	6.5%
Copper	0.5%
Cobalt	1/10%

Firing

Best result for this glaze is
1260–1280°C
(2300–2336°F) gas
reduction firing
Reducing from 1000–1200°C
(1832–2192°F)

1 Throw a bowl with straight, almost upright, sides, 25 cm (10 in) taller than you require, leaving a wide base. This bowl should have a thick rim and base because at a later stage it will be turned over and rested on its rim while you work on the base.

2 Throw the rim to a surface depth of 25 cm (10 in) leaning 45 degrees towards the centre of the bowl. Flatten the rim with a kidney, supporting it from the inside. Draw a line around the bottom of the rim. This will stop the manganese dioxide, applied later, from running down the side of the bowl. Finish off with soft plastic – an old credit or phone card will not get rusty or cut you when it gets worn.

3 While throwing leg cylinders, keep the base narrow and the rim quite thin. Slowly collar in from the base upwards. Do not close the opening because air inside may distort the shape.

4 When you have the desired angle, smooth with a kidney. Compress the tip to close the cone. Draw horizontal guidelines and then cut the leg off the board for drying. Repeat twice.

5 When the bowl is leatherhard, turn the base into a dome reflecting the shape inside. It is best to turn this shape from the rim to the base.

6 Draw guidelines for the decoration of the bowl and legs. This process is much more easily executed on the wheel.

7 Measure the correct position for the legs. Stick on the legs temporarily with slip. Mark around them with a tool. Remove the legs then score and slurry the bowl and legs where they are to meet. Replace and fix the legs firmly and finish off with a paintbrush.

8 Draw the surface decoration on the bowl. Then put a needle hole in each of the legs, otherwise they may crack when drying or explode during biscuit firing. Leave the bowl to dry upside-down to stop warping then slow biscuit (bisque) fire it to 1000°C (1832°F) or 06 cone.

9 Paint on the manganese dioxide and when it is dry, sponge off the surplus. There will be enough left in the grooves to melt the covering layer of glaze.

10 Pour the glaze inside the bowl first. Try to get different thicknesses with the glaze. This glaze breaks into three colours, so the colours can be very dramatic.

11 Place the bowl upside-down over a glaze rack and basin. Pour glaze on the outside, again varying the thickness for the best effects.

12 When the glaze has dried clean off the rim with a kidney and sponge. Apply manganese dioxide to the rim with a brush using a banding wheel. Wipe the feet and put sand on your kiln shelves to stop the bowl sticking to their surface. Fire the bowl. The reduction within this firing cycle will bring the iron speckle to the surface of the clay, giving you a blue, green and yellow dry to satin-matt surface.

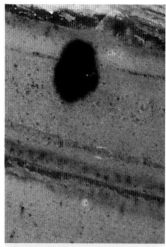

Teapot

Tea drinking originated in the Far East and beautiful variations of the teapot's ergonomic form, with handles made from clay, cane or metal can be seen in many museum collections. The three thrown elements of body, lid and spout in this piece by Richard Phethean combine harmoniously to create a lightweight, functional and aesthetic form. The same basic process can be adapted to follow different teapot designs.

Materials
Spencroft sanded red
    earthenware "green dot"

Equipment
Wheel and cutting wire
Bat
Rib
Callipers
Metal tool
Wire or tough cotton
Round stick
Metal kidney
Tool to bore straining holes
Serrated metal kidney
Toothbrush
Plastic
Potter's knife
Wax resist
Gloves for glazing
Brushes for slip
Electric kiln

Slips
White – white Devon ball clay
Light blue – add 5% cobalt
    oxide
Dark blue – add 20% cobalt
    oxide
Watery green – add 10%
    copper oxide and 1%
    chrome oxide
Thin blue/black lines – neat
    cobalt oxide
Make up the coloured slips to
a thin watery consistency

Glaze
CLEAR
Lead bisilicate	72%
Potash feldspar	13%
Ball clay	10%
Borax frit	5%
Bentonite	2%

HONEY
Powdered red earthenware
    clay is substituted for ball
    clay in above recipe
Red iron oxide   ½%

Firing
Biscuit (bisque) fire to 1050°C
    (1922°F)
Glaze fire to 1125°C
    (2057°F), cones 03/02

1 Centre 900 g (2 lb) of clay into a shallow dome about 16–18 cm (6¼–7 in) wide to make the body. Open out the base as you would a flat plate with a thickness of 4 mm (⅙ in). Lift the wall into a tall, even cone leaving a little weight on the collar rim.

2 At a gentle speed, keep the aperture of the neck just narrow enough to admit your hand and gently stroke out the form into a cylinder against the rib. Collar in the top third of the form to a quarter of the cone.

3 Support under the shoulder while the rib leans down on top, closing the diameter of the neck and creating a subtle step to the rim. Then create combed detail with a serrated metal kidney.

4 Cut a decorative, "spiral" crease with the corner of the rib. Finally, measure the neck's aperture with a pair of callipers with the points facing each other. Dry to leatherhard.

5 The lid is thrown "off the hump" so centre 1 kg (2¼ lb) of clay into an upright cone, then create a "waist" below sufficient clay to make your lid. Hollow "off-centre" with one finger to create a knob and tuck the other finger into the waistline to pinch out a shallow "saucer".

6 Refine the knob with two fingers of one hand, and fold over the rim of the saucer creating a flange to sit on the rim of the teapot. Use the callipers to check the width of the lid underneath the flange.

7 Cut a V-shaped groove to clearly divide the lid from the hump. Cut the lid from the hump with either a cutting wire or a length of tough cotton looped around the groove and held at one end as the wheel rotates slowly. The latter always makes a neat horizontal cut. Wait until the lid has dried to leatherhard.

8 Use the same hump to recentre and recreate a "waisted" ball for the spout. Hollow and deeply undercut the base of a small cone to make quite sure that all the available clay is utilized.

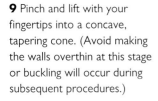

9 Pinch and lift with your fingertips into a concave, tapering cone. (Avoid making the walls overthin at this stage or buckling will occur during subsequent procedures.)

10 Use an upward, collaring action to close up the spout a little, creating a wide skirt and a long, narrow neck.

11 Pinch against a round stick to further raise and thin the spout's neck. The slender, parallel neck should be almost as tall as the flared cone it sits on.

12 Refine the line and surface of the spout with a rib or metal kidney, then underscore the completed spout. Cut through with a cutting wire and remove it with its own base. Preserve the spout in a softer state than the teapot body and lid.

13 Trim and refine the teapot body and the lid. Then cut the spout from its base at a diagonal angle with a cutting wire. Gently pick up the soft spout and, with a wet finger, moisten and slightly flare the joining edge. Offer the spout up to the pot and lightly touch it into position.

14 Replace the spout on its base while you bore the straining holes within the mark left by the spout. Make as many holes as you can. Textured decoration can be added with a serrated metal kidney.

15 Use a wet toothbrush to roughen the pot around the straining holes. Pick up the spout and roughen its joining edge as well. Position the spout directly over the strainer and gently press into place. Carefully blend the spout seamlessly into the wall of the teapot.

16 Extrude a strap handle (see extruding handles), allow it to stiffen and then trim it to the desired length. Score and slurry the ends of the strap and teapot where the handle will be fitted. Hold the strap vertically and pinch and weld the front end into position. Add a decorative finish to the handle with the serrated metal kidney.

17 Loop the strap over a hand and weld it at the other end. Take care to align it accurately with the spout. Replace the lid and wrap the teapot in plastic, allowing all the elements of the finished teapot to equalize to a leatherhard state.

18 Next trim the spout with a sharp knife blade for length, and angle it to make a crisp pouring lip. To jet nicely, the spout must have a good funnel shape, compressing and speeding up the water flow, and the lid must have a small hole cut into it to allow air into the pot as the tea comes out.

19 Allow the pot to dry, ensuring that the handle and spout equalize to the same condition as the pot, by covering them in plastic for a day or so. Brush areas to be protected from slip coating with wax resist. Dip the teapot, rim first into the white slip. Gently shake the drips off and stand upright to dry. Apply the coloured slips. Biscuit (bisque) fire and glaze and fire.

Porcelain Bowl

Sue Paraskeva, the maker of this thrown porcelain vessel, sees the stick-driven momentum wheel as an important part of the making process as it is beautifully simple and encourages good pottery. After throwing, the vessel is slowly dried and carved, reshaping the base and altering the balance. Inspired by the natural form of pebbles, particularly their decoration and the shadows they create, some of her pieces are raw glazed with classical porcelain glazes, others are thrown with various oxides, grogs and other decoration materials.

Materials

1 kg (2¼ lb) Limoges Porcelain

Equipment

Stick-driven momentum wheel
Strong cutting wire
Fine cutting wire
Sponge
Firm rubber kidney
Strip of chamois leather
Metal tool
Wooden bat
Newspaper squares
Small surform blade
Plastic sheet
Hacksaw blades
Old-fashioned razor blades
Paintbrush
Gloves for glazing
Wax resist
Large bowl
Jug (pitcher)
Gas-fired kiln

Glaze

Celadon glaze based on a
    recipe by John Davis

Potash feldspar	42%
Quartz	27%
Wolsanite	17%
China clay	13%
Red iron oxide	2%

Firing

Reduction fired to 1260°C
    (2300°F)

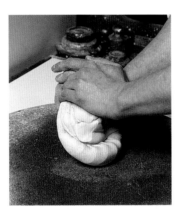

1 Make sure the clay is well mixed with an even consistency. Spiral wedging is a good final preparation before going to the wheel. Pat the porcelain into a ball, place it firmly in the centre of the wheelhead then wind up the wheel.

2 Once it is spinning, wet both hands and place them firmly on either side of the ball. Apply downward pressure and a cone will begin to rise in the centre. Press the cone harder and it will spiral upwards.

3 Place your hands, interlinked, over the top of the cone and push gently downward. Apply some inwards pressure to keep the clay central and bring the clay down into a mushroom shape. Now it is centred and ready to make into a pot.

4 Splash some more water onto the clay with one hand around the back of the pot. Then, with your other hand over the top, place your thumb over the centre. Push your thumb down into the middle of the clay, making sure to use enough water so that it doesn't get too sticky.

5 Push down, leaving enough clay at the bottom for the base, and swing your thumb firmly from side to side to define the curve of the pot. Use the other hand for support so that the porcelain does not flare out.

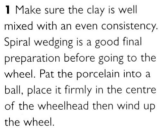

6 Next, pull up the wall of the pot. With one hand inside and one outside, use your fingertips to lift (pull) a collar of clay from the base of the pot to the top. Do this steadily and repeatedly. If you are using a non-electric wheel make sure you are not pulling up the clay faster than the revolutions of the wheel.

7 Repeat this process until the walls are as high as required, then begin to flare out the pot. Always start at the bottom and work up to the very top. Use a sponge or a kidney-shaped tool to use all the clay and to reveal the smoothness of the porcelain.

8 Slow down electric wheels considerably at this stage (momentum wheels will have slowed down naturally at this point). Using a rubber kidney on the inside, continue flaring out the pot, concentrating particularly on the inside of the form. Because you are making a fine bowl, the outside shape will follow the inside form.

9 Check that the rim is smooth and even. Do this very gently with your fingers and then use a small slither of wet chamois leather to finish.

10 The pot is finished. Clean the base with a sharp tool, cutting in slightly, then stop the wheel. Sponge some water on the wheelhead at the back of the pot and pull a fine cutting wire through under the pot to release it from the wheel. Always use clean water and pull the wire through three times to make certain of a clean release. Cover a bat with newspaper then pick up the pot and place it on the bat. This facilitates even drying and eliminates the need for further cutting.

11 Leave the pot to dry overnight and when it is firm enough to handle, begin to carve back the base using a small surform blade. As soon as you feel the softer clay underneath, stop work. Wrap the pot in plastic and leave it overnight to firm up. Wrapping the pot in this way ensures a slow and even drying process.

12 The next day, when the pot has firmed again, carve it back with a more delicate hacksaw blade to get the detail of the final shape. Again, leave it wrapped overnight.

13 Take a razor blade or a sharp metal kidney to get rid of the texture lines. Make the base flat, or angle the pot as desired. Allow the pot to dry fully when finished.

14 Brush wax-resist inside the rim and on the base. This will repel any glaze on areas to be left unglazed. Because the pot is unfired or raw, sponging back will only disturb the form.

15 Wearing gloves, hold the pot very carefully, upside down, over a large bowl then pour the glaze evenly all over the pot. The piece is at its most fragile at this point, so carefully wipe back any drips before gently setting it down to dry.

16 Pack the pot into the kiln when it is dry. Create the green celadon glaze from iron oxide by firing in a reduced atmosphere. No biscuit (bisque) firing is needed as the pot is fired raw. The firing takes 11 hours to reach 1260°C (2300°F).

Undulating Vase

This throwing project is inspired by the quote by Lao Tzu, "it is written the water that flows into the earthenware vessel takes on its form". Nicholas Arroyave~Portela's interest in this form lies in the accentuation of throwing lines, the rethrowing of the pot at various intervals to make the clay walls as thin as possible, drying it out with a paint stripper gun in order to continue working it and, finally, its tactile manipulation.

Materials

1 kg (2¼ lb) ball white St Thomas clay

Equipment

Electric wheel and serrated wire cutter
Wooden bats
Sponges of different sizes
Needle
Wooden tool
Paint stripper gun
Water spray
Plastic sheet
Spray booth
Face mask (respirator)
Gloves for glazing
Sandpaper (medium-coarse)
Banding wheel
Newspaper
Compressor
Spray gun
Electric kiln and controller

Slip

TERRA SIGILLATA
3 litres (5¼ pt) warm water
1 kg (2¼ lb) dry white ball clay hymod
15 g (½ oz) Hexametaphosphate
8%–10% commercial stains
1%–10% oxides
Ball mill the Hexametaphosphate with the water, oxide and/or stain.

Glaze

Ready-made transparent glaze CT2330, range 1110–1180°C (2030–2156°F)
Oxides 1%–4% (different coloured glazes on different slips will have different effects)

Firing

1000°C (1832°F)
60°C (140°F) an hour until 300°C (572°F)
120°C (248°F) an hour until 1000°C (1832°F)
5 minute soak at 1000°C (1832°F)

1180°C (2156°F)
60°C (140°F) an hour until 300°C (572°F)
120°C (248°F) an hour until 1180°C (2156°F)
10 minute soak at 1180°C (2156°F)

1 Have a bowl of water, a sponge, cutting wire, a needle and a sharp wooden tool ready before you start work. Put the clay on the wheel and centre it. Begin to spin the wheel.

2 Start to draw up the clay. Try to even out the clay walls by continual throwing, starting upwards from the thickest at the bottom, but be very careful not to tire the clay out too quickly.

3 Once you have some height, start to define the shape of the vase by pushing out the main body, then pulling it back in at the shoulder before flaring out the rim.

4 Now the clay probably needs some drying out with the paint stripper gun. Carry this out evenly while the wheelhead turns slowly. Slightly wobble the appliance up and down so that no patch of the pot is overly exposed to the direct heat.

5 Take away some of the excess clay at the bottom of the pot with a sharp wooden tool. This clay usually proves difficult to lose completely in the throwing process.

6 Use the water spray when rethrowing the pot so as not to oversaturate it. Push out the final shape of the main body, making sure that the clay walls are thin enough to manipulate.

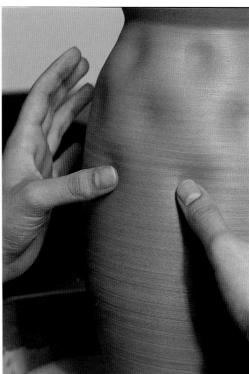

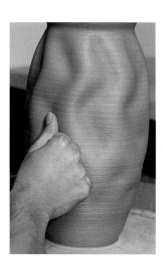

9 Join the undulations with your thumb and start to create a zigzag definition.

7 Refine the rim by softening any sharp edges with a sponge at a slow and constant speed. This is the final stage of throwing the vase.

10 This pattern is effective when viewed from the inside too. Free the bottom of the pot from the bat with serrated wire and cover it lightly with some plastic for a day. Then remove the sheeting to allow it to dry. This may take up to a week.

8 Touch the pot to see that it is not too wet nor too dry, then lightly indent the surface of the pot with your thumbs, maintaining a regularity around the whole pot from the top to the bottom.

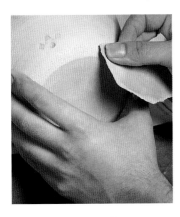

11 Place the bone-dry pot on its side on a large sponge in the spray booth then, while wearing a face mask (respirator), gently remove any sharp edges with a piece of medium-coarse sandpaper. Be sure to sand away the same amount around the whole pot to maintain its regularity. Aim also to taper the line in at the bottom. This will give the desired effect of lift to the pot once it is standing.

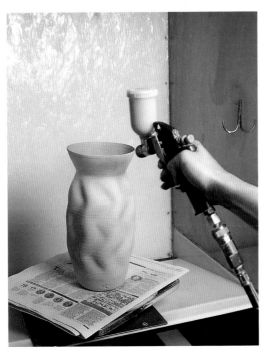

12 Place the pot on a banding wheel covered with newspaper. Then, while wearing your face mask, spray the slip evenly around the pot from top to bottom, turning the wheel intermittently.

13 Give the piece about three coats of slip with a break of a couple of hours between each layer. Remember – the pot is not fired so it will crack if oversaturated.

14 Place the pot back on its side once it has dried sufficiently after its three layers of slip. Take a different coloured slip, spray it across the bottom of the pot and let the contrast catch on the throwing lines and shape. Make sure you keep turning the pot after each spray so that the same effect can be seen all the way round. Leave for a day to dry, then fire the piece to 1000°C (1832°F).

15 Pour the slip into the fired pot and give the inside a good coating, making sure that all the areas are covered. Pour out the slip to ensure that the inside rim gets coated as well. Let the pot dry for a day, then do the same with the glaze, being careful not to spill any on the outer surface. The glaze must have a thin consistency so that it does not go on too thickly.

16 Finally, clean any spillage off the outside of the pot with warm water and a sponge (you will have to change the water regularly). Wipe the edges clear with a small sponge to reveal a clear line between glaze and slip. Leave your vase for a day before firing to 1180°C (1976°F).

INDEX

Author's acknowledgements
Many thanks to all those who gave help with the arrangements for photography and to those who have contributed project work.
Richard Phethean for his chapter and projects on throwing methods and David Richardson for his contributions and advice regarding plaster working methods. Stephen Brayne for his creative photographic documentation of techniques and project work as well as his fearless exposure to shooting flames and searing heat.
Emma Clegg for giving me this opportunity to consolidate and learn and for always being there on telephone or fax to calmly guide me through the book-making process.
Nigel Hubbers for advice about the use of internet; Steve Rafferty of Ceramatech for swift organising and delivery of materials; Teresa Pateman for the loan of etching plates; Pip Cronin and Jessica Cohen for the use of their studio and equipment; Chris Bramble and Kay Suckling for their preparation work for photography; David Bailey Junior at Longton Light Alloys for their speedy supply of extruding equipment; Iain Ogilvie at Blackthorn Galleries for selling advice; Jonathan Knowles, Yiolanda Christou and Billy Nicholas for kiln watching; Vince Woodrush for backdrop and light; and Maria Donato for supplying printing blocks and equipment.
My thanks are due also to Daphne Carnegy as adviser on glaze technicalities and as book writing mentor; John Forde for acting as consultant; Jenny Lomax and Laurie Peake and the entire Camden Arts centre team past and present for my much enjoyed teaching opportunities and enlightenment.
Many thanks to Dorcas Apoh for entertaining and caring for my son while I met the deadline. And to my partner Peter Norman for all his encouragement and support, as well as help and advice with the keyboard.